WESTERN MEDIA NARRATIVES ON INDIA

'Umesh Upadhyay, through his book based on rigorous research, has convincingly shown how the Western media has traditionally been biased and negative, projecting a distorted image of India. These lopsided images now appear to be contradictory to India's stature as an emerging twenty-first-century global power in this technology-driven world. Upadhyay has very rightly pointed out that the credibility of the Western media will be at stake if it does not change its approach towards India. This book is indeed a very interesting and informative study.'

Harivansh

Deputy chairman, Rajya Sabha

'Global narratives, including external perceptions of India, have been thus far driven exclusively by the Western media for its own purposes. In this very readable book, Umesh Upadhyay recounts, with clarity and undeniable evidence, the history of how this skewed media narrative has been used to box India's place in the world since 1947. It then makes the case for a rising India to tell its own story.'

Sanjeev Sanyal

Economist and bestselling author

'It is obvious to any Indian that the Western media is biased against us. But simply reacting emotionally to their biases is not going to help us. To address a problem, we must first understand it. Umesh Upadhyay offers a calm and clinical analysis of the Western media in the book. For all those who are frustrated with Western media, and how it often creates problems in India's relations with Western countries, this is a must-read.'

Amish Tripathi

Bestselling author

WESTERN MEDIA NARRATIVES ON INDIA

FROM GANDHI TO MODI

UMESH UPADHYAY

RUPA

Published by
Rupa Publications India Pvt. Ltd 2024
7/16, Ansari Road, Daryaganj
New Delhi 110002

Sales centres:
Bengaluru Chennai Hyderabad
Jaipur Kathmandu Kolkata
Mumbai Prayagraj

P-ISBN: 978-93-90260-94-2
E-ISBN: 978-93-90260-64-5

First impression 2024

10 9 8 7 6 5 4 3 2 1

Printed in India

My first book is dedicated to my revered Mataji and Pitaji, who not only bestowed upon me the gift of life but also imparted the wisdom to navigate its intricacies; my esteemed Bade Bhaisahab, whose guidance illuminated the significance of education and knowledge; and my revered Guruji, whose teachings continue to illuminate the profound essence of life for me.

CONTENTS

Foreword *ix*
Preface *xi*

1. It's an Old Story 1

2. Western Media in Post-Independence India 24

3. Indira or Atal, Doesn't Matter 45

4. The Elite Space Club 63

5. Covid-19: A Modi-Bashing Event by the Western Media 80

6. India Still a Land of Snake Charmers? 124

7. Colonization of Minds 138

Annexure: Articles with Biased Content against India 154
Index 160

FOREWORD

Umesh Upadhyay's book, *Western Media Narratives on India: From Gandhi to Modi,* is an analytical study seeking to highlight the decades-old bias of the Western media in its slanted coverage of developments in India. Starting from Mahatma Gandhi to Prime Minister Shri Narendra Modi, Upadhyay draws the reader's attention to various narratives built on half-truths by the Western media over time. He traces how this long tradition of biased coverage of India has become more pronounced during crises such as Covid-19. He lays bare how, in its reportage of Bharat, the dominant Western English media deliberately belittles India's achievements and magnifies fault lines and calamities.

The book delves into the historical background of the Western media's perception of India, starting from colonial times and subsequent periods after Independence. It reveals how leaders such as Mahatma Gandhi, Sardar Vallabhbhai Patel, Dr B.R. Ambedkar, Jawaharlal Nehru, Indira Gandhi and Atal Bihari Vajpayee have been targeted by the English media on various occasions. Upadhyay exposes the seamless manner in which the narrative building by the dominant

Western English media continues even in the age of social and digital media.

It is widely believed that the elite of the Western powers have used the media as a tool to target most developing societies, including India. The media, it is said, is used to strengthen the existing geopolitical power balance in the world. A new world information order built on greater objectivity and impartiality is set to emerge, especially when the credibility of some of the so-called leading media outlets has become questionable.

Upadhyay employs a multi-disciplinary approach, drawing on various fields such as media studies, history, sociology and political science, as also a variety of sources such as news articles, speeches, books, studies, research findings and sample surveys to analyse the Western media's coverage of India in particular and other developing societies in general. The book also uses a critical lens to examine how the Western media's narrative of India is shaped by their own biases and worldviews.

Umesh Upadhyay's long years of experience in the media comes in handy to dissect news reports and reveal diverse facets which colour coverage sported by the Western media. This book serves as a handbook or eye-opener to Indian media houses- it gives them food for thought to put Bharat first.

18 December 2023 — M. Venkaiah Naidu
Hyderabad — Former Vice President of India

PREFACE

My interest in study of the Western media is quite old. It started when I was studying International Relations at the School of International Studies, Jawaharlal Nehru University (JNU), New Delhi, in the early 1980s. In the summer of1982, during my master's, I happened to visit Canada. That was when Punjab was going through a very difficult time. A section of the Sikhs had taken to militancy in the state. The former chief minister (CM) of Punjab, Giani Zail Singh, was the home minister of India. Later, in July 1982, he was elected the seventh president of India. As I was in Canada for four months, I had assumed that this news would find a place in local Canadian newspapers sooner or later. To my utter surprise, there was no mention of India having a new president in the Canadian newspapers I subscribed to.

Even back then, Canada had a sizable Punjabi population, so much so that some signage in certain areas was in Gurmukhi. If you happened to travel by Air Canada, there were announcements in Punjabi. Thus, I had assumed that the appointment of the first Sikh president of India would find at least a mention in the local newspapers there, but my assumption was proven wrong.

One day, I finally found a news article about India in the local Canadian newspapers. It was regarding a bus tragedy. Some Hindu pilgrims had been killed when the bus they were travelling slipped into a *khud* (a deep ravine). A bus accident in India finds a place in the international section of a Canadian newspaper, but the world's largest democracy getting a new president—that too a Sikh—doesn't. *Why is that?* This question kept bothering me for a long time.

Over the last four decades, I have travelled to many nations, including the United States of America (USA), United Kingdom (UK) and Canada. It has struck me that India features in the newspapers of these countries only if there is a tragedy, political upheaval or violence. I wanted to study this phenomenon for my doctorate in JNU, but I got a job as a journalist and decided not to pursue further studies. But the Western media's coverage of India and its impact and influence continued to fascinate me, and as a journalist, I kept a careful, close watch on the coverage over the years.

I believe that the fundamental issue with the Western media's coverage of developing countries like India is that it solely focusses on disasters—manmade or natural. It creates a lopsided image of such countries as crisis-ridden nations. This image is created in the developed world for local populations as well as the diaspora living there.

The opinion of local populations on international events covered by the Western media is very important as it leads to creation of biases and prejudices. Let me quote a case about the Iron Man of India, Sardar Vallabhbhai Patel. Sardar Patel is considered the architect of the modern Indian State. He integrated hundreds of princely states into India. He has been described as Bismarck of India by many, including habitual anti-India bashers like Winston Churchill, for his efforts towards uniting India.[1] However, an altogether different picture of Sardar Patel was painted by the British press that described him as a villain during early days of India's independence.

A letter written by one Gordon Collyer, a commoner living in London, is a testimony to how agenda-driven reporting distorts image. Collyer read the reports published in the British media about Sardar Patel's integration of princely states, especially Hyderabad. Back then, newspapers had been publishing one-sided reports, describing Sardar Patel as a trouble-maker in Hyderabad who was not abiding by the standstill agreement entered into with the Nizam of the princely state. However, there was more nuance to the situation that the British news reports accounted for.[2]

These lopsided reports in the media were then used to raise the issue in British Parliament. Collyer, after having read the reports, wrote a letter to Sardar Patel stating that he did not like the way the Indian home minister had dealt with the issue. The letter described the Nizam as the victim and Patel as an oppressor and a bully. Collyer did not expect a reply from Patel, who had also been appointed as the first deputy prime minister (PM) of India. However, Patel replied with a long letter, in which he categorically said that '[w]e have ample evidence of British Press correspondents in this country deliberately misrepresenting both factually and ideologically'.[3]

---

[1]Phukan, Parag, 'Sardar Patel: Bismarck of India', *Sentinel*, 3 November 2023, https://tinyurl.com/nhm2fnt4. Accessed on 27 September 2023.

[2]Das, Durga (ed.), *Sardar Patel's Correspondence: 1945–50,* Volume 6, Navajivan Publishing House, Ahmedabad, 1973, p. 456.

[3]Ibid.

Even Mahatma Gandhi was also not spared from rumours by the British press in India. He was dismayed to find media reports published in December 1947 stating that he and Sardar Patel were so tired that they were planning a sojourn in Pilani, Rajasthan, to rest.[4] Seeing some of the reports, the first PM of India, Jawaharlal Nehru, remarked that Reuters was an out-and-out British news agency and its reporters posted in Pakistan carried out anti-India propaganda.[5] There was a deliberate attempt to denigrate Indian leaders such as Gandhi, Patel and Dr B.R. Ambedkar in the media. It only proves that India and its leadership have been targeted with half-truths right from the beginning. The same happened with Indira Gandhi and Atal Bihari Vajpayee.

This agenda-driven reporting against India has continued unabated. It is clear from the way the prominent UK and US newspapers covered Covid-19. I had started following closely the Western media's Covid-19 coverage from March 2020. It was the time when the pandemic had already started playing havoc in Europe and the USA. The number of Covid-19 infection cases in India was still in hundreds back then.[6] However, Western media houses started speculating about what will happen when the virus strikes India.

It was intriguing to find many of these reports comparing what happened in India during the Spanish Flu in 1918–20.

---

[4]Gandhi, M.K., *The Collected Works of Mahatma Gandhi*, Publications Division, Ministry of Information and Broadcasting, Government of India, 1989, p. 200.

[5]S. Gopal (ed.), *Selected Works of Jawaharlal Nehru*, Volume 19, Second Series, Jawaharlal Nehru Memorial Fund, New Delhi, p. 181.

[6]'India Coronavirus Lockdown I Day 1 Updates March 25, 2020', *Hindu*, 25 March 2020, https://tinyurl.com/3ay9ra4u. Accessed on 27 September 2023.

Some of the media went too far and a few of the Western newspapers claimed that Mahatma Gandhi also was infected by the dreaded Spanish Flu in August 1918.[7] This news was copied and reproduced by many other international and local publications, and no one bothered to check facts. The media echoed each other and fell into the trap of reporting misleading articles. Unfortunately, this is how the international news networks operate. In this book, we debunk this misinformation and prove that Gandhi did not catch the Spanish Flu.

It was estimated that 17–18 million Indians died due to the Spanish Flu during the last century.[8] While there is no issue in mentioning the numbers of Indians who lost lives due to the Flu and in the Bengal famine of 1943 as historical facts, it was surely unfair to allude that the same may happen in 2020 during Covid-19, which many media reports did.[9] Some reports almost habitually mentioned Spanish Flu deaths in India while reporting on Covid-19. This was a rather unscientific way to set a narrative with an overwhelmingly anti-India overtone. When experts were

---

[7]Morrison, Pat, 'Column: What the Deadly 1918 Flu Epidemic Can Teach Us about Our Coronavirus Reaction', *Los Angeles Times*, 11 March 2020, https://tinyurl.com/3an64a8j. Accessed on 27 September 2023.

[8]Spinney, Laura, *Pale Rider: Spanish Flu of 1918 and How It Changed the World*, PublicAffairs, New York, 2017, p. 116.

[9]Menezes, Vivek, 'India's Leaders Have Panicked. Now the Millions Who Power the Country Are Suffering', *Guardian*, 8 April 2020, https://tinyurl.com/34afwh98. Accessed on 1 December; Ellis-Petersen, Hannah, 'Reporting from India: "Pandemics have a Painful Legacy Here"', *Guardian*, 13 September 2020, http://tinyurl.com/mr2czb25. Accessed on 3 January 2024; Satam, Mrunmayee, 'India's Worst Affected: The Socio-economic Parallels between Influenza (1918–19) and Covid-19 in Mumbai', *History and Policy*, 24 June 2020, http://tinyurl.com/2hm74hpx. Accessed on 3 January 2024.

not sure of what shape the disease may take, why should journalists have forecast what was likely to happen in India during Covid-19 or how many people will die? Thankfully, all these doomsday predictions and negative prophecies were proven wrong.

The more I read, the more I realized that Covid-19 was another lost opportunity for the Western media so far as India was concerned. The Western media used it as just another case where they could further cement their long-held prejudicial view that India was chaotic, poor, unorganized, unhygienic and ungovernable, and its administrative system was incapable of managing itself.

Many Western publications had already declared PM Narendra Modi a 'Hindu nationalist' and his government as a Hindu nationalist government.[10] So, they believed that the government could do nothing right. Thus, rather than the factual reporting, they started cherry picking the stories that suited their assumed beliefs. Many of them did stories based on hearsay, unconfirmed reports and unverified data. Later, they used the pandemic to further their anti-Modi agenda as well.

In May 2021, the *New York Times* declared that Covid-19 could potentially take the lives of 4.2 million Indians.[11] These calculated estimates of casualty numbers are nowhere near the actual toll of 0.53 million deaths reported till May

---

[10]Gowen, Annie, 'Hindu Nationalist Narendra Modi Sworn in as India's Prime Minister', *Washington Post*, 26 May 2014, https://tinyurl.com/72kvsrk9. Accessed on 1 December 2023.

[11]Gamio, Lazaro and James Glanz, 'Just How Big Could India's Covid Toll Be?', *New York Times*, 25 May 2021, http://tinyurl.com/3j32j7cp. Accessed on 3 January 2024.

2023.[12] The *New York Times* was probably a victim of its own propaganda of not believing the official data released by the Government of India (GoI). It ran a series of stories doubting the government data, and while doing so, became insensitive enough to speculate on the deaths of Indian citizens.

∽

For this book, we studied some 230 articles and news items published by major UK and US English publications from March 2020 to June 2021. These were the toughest months for the country as the period included the first two waves of the pandemic. Most of the devastation caused by the disease occurred during this period. These were selected using a random sample method. Articles were taken from websites of the selected publications. We tried to dive deep into how the mainstream British and US English media covered Covid-19 situations in India for the first 15 months of the pandemic. The detailed analysis of the same is presented in one of the chapters.

I wish to add here that as editors of news channels, newspapers, news websites, etc., we decide our priorities. Which story will be our cover story, what will go to inside pages, what angle we will choose to present the story from—these are all subjective decisions. Journalists take these editorial calls all the time. Yet, we are all bound by some basic principles of journalism. It is when there are constant departures from the universally agreed norms that coverages stand out as biased or agenda-driven.

---

[12]'COVID-19 Coronavirus Pandemic', *Worldometer*, http://tinyurl.com/buhppr2n. Accessed on 27 September 2023.

Sadly, the international media outfits don't really pass with flying colours when one looks at the articles and commentaries during the specified period. It is also a sad commentary on the news ecosystem which reproduced many of these reports without verifying and rechecking. It was interesting to see how these publications cross-reference each other without checking the sources.

Covid-19 was not a time when the Western media should have played games with the narrative. It was an opportunity for it to redeem itself with factual, empathetic content and reporting that was sensitive towards the people of India. The pandemic was as tragic for India as it was for any other country. But, as they say, old habits die hard. In their efforts to somehow paint Modi government black, they often forgot their essential and fundamental obligation towards their readers, which was to provide them with correct factual information. This was the time to arm people with information to combat the pandemic effectively. Yet, instead of giving the readers hope, belief and confidence during the challenging time, the Western media dished out fear, hopelessness and despair. Given the data, India did better than it was predicted to, and some credit was surely due to its leadership. However, the Western media did not want to acknowledge that the Modi government did well to fight the pandemic and, hence, the negative Covid-19 reporting.

While dealing with the issue of narrative building by the Western media, I have drawn heavily from history. As a disclaimer, I wish to declare that I am not a historian but have only looked at historical events from the perspective of a commoner or a journalist at best. I have drawn heavily from media reports and other documented sources out of my curiosity. My experience in various newsrooms as a journalist has helped me analyse events and happenings, especially during the pandemic days, from readers' perspective rather than an expert point of view. I am not too sure of the experts' opinion but hope that common readers will find some value in my research and efforts.

Chapter 1

IT'S AN OLD STORY

Suriname, a country in South America, gained independence from Dutch rule on 25 November 1975. Strangely, no South American newspaper sent a reporter to cover this seminal event in their neighbourhood,[1] and none of them thought it fit to publish this news on their front pages, even though Suriname is an important country on the continent.

The importance of Suriname can be gauged from a very interesting historical fact. When Britain and the Netherlands signed the Treaty of Breda in 1667 after the second Anglo-Dutch war, the Dutch settled in Suriname instead of New York, which was called the New Amsterdam back then.

Suriname was an important source of sugar with its huge sugarcane plantations. It also had gold mines, so the Dutch were more interested in keeping it under their thumb than keeping New Amsterdam. In a nutshell, the Netherlands, in

[1]Smith, Anthony, *The Geopolitics of Information: How Western Culture Dominates the World*, Faber and Faber, London, 1980, p. 71.

the seventeenth century, thought that Suriname was more important than New York. Even in later years, it continued as an important source of oil and bauxite. It was one of the major exporters of bauxite to the USA during World War II. In fact, Suriname, along with its immediate neighbour Guyana, has the largest bauxite deposit in the world. In the light of Suriname's significance, it is surprising, then, that the South American media did not take cognizance of an important moment in the country's history.

A VEIL OF SILENCE ON SURINAME

Why did the media in its immediate South American neighbourhood not give any importance to the news of Suriname's independence? We are talking of the mid-1970s. These were the days when the Non-Aligned Movement (NAM) was very actively trying to establish a New World Information Order (NWIO) to fight the colonial and imperialist mindset of the West, as most South American nations had faced European imperialism and had a colonial past. Many Latin American countries were active in the NAM, which Suriname later joined. Being a South American nation, to Suriname, the US media mattered the most. While the attitude of the mainstream US and other Western media was not expected to be of empathy towards one of the Third-World countries breaking out of the clutches of imperialism, it was naturally expected that when a fellow nation finally got independence, the media of neighbouring nations will cover it prominently, if not joining the celebrations.

A Mexican researcher, Fernando Reyes Matta, did an interesting case study on the coverage of the independence of Suriname.[2] He concluded that it was not perceived as an important event for news coverage because the Latin American press normally operated in a 'receive-only' mode towards international news and accepted the worldview of its principal news suppliers, that is, the Western media. Therefore, any country that was not considered important or significant by US journalists was ignored. The entire Latin American press followed the US media. It would ignore events even in their own countries if the US journalists found them not relevant.[3]

The famous Brazilian paper *O Estado* did cover the news of Suriname's independence, but it was confined to an inside page. Significantly, the paper carried an agency copy written by a US journalist as a three-column story. Events of much less magnitude in any of the US cities, such as New York, Chicago or San Francisco, would possibly have got more space in the paper than the story of Suriname's independence. There is no point in guessing that the story was written in a similar negative tone and carried the familiar narrative as the British had about India—that Suriname was incapable of governing itself; that there would be ethnic and racial conflicts in the immediate future; that it would not be able to hold itself together, etc. Is it not ironic that even though Brazil shares a border with Suriname, its influential newspapers thought it prudent to carry the US narrative for its neighbour on a day of huge historical importance rather than sending a reporter across the border?

---

[2]Matta, F.R., 'The Latin American Concept of News', *Journal of Communication*, Volume 29, No. 2, 1979, pp. 164–71.
[3]Ibid.

This is not an isolated incident. This explicit insensitivity towards neighbouring societies is a result of the inbuilt mechanism of news gathering and dissemination. We usually read more about what is happening in the Western world rather than in our immediate neighbourhood countries. The media outlets in developing countries invariably give prominent space to what is happening in the USA, Europe or other Western countries. The private lives of Hollywood celebrities, models, fashion designers, the UK's royal family, American politicians, businessmen, tech companies, media barons, sportspersons and related events are given the same space as when covering their own celebrities. However, such people and events in other parts of Asia, Africa and Latin America seldom find any significant mention in the local media. Almost all developing societies face a similar situation. The problem is in the origin of news, the training of journalists and the larger ecosystem of information that has been built over the years. The evolution of modern media is part of the process of colonization.

EUROPEAN EXPEDITIONS

When European explorers set out to discover the world and new trade routes, they mostly represented the commercial interests of those who had invested in these costly and often very arduous voyages. Investors in these expeditions needed information about the new markets out there. Many joint-stock companies were launched in Europe to exploit the colonies' resources to the maximum. When Christopher Columbus set sail in 1492 from Spain, his idea was to discover a sea route to Asia for the lucrative spice trade. He only accidentally discovered America. He called the natives *indios* (Indians)—the derogatory nomenclature that is still used for the aboriginals in the USA and Canada, though very few of them survive today. Columbus's expeditions started a period of exploration, conquest, loot, annihilation of natives and colonization that lasted for centuries.

Ultimately, it was the Portuguese explorer Vasco da Gama who discovered the sea route to India (1497–99) on a voyage funded by the then monarch, King Manuel I. In 1500, the monarch reorganized the royal trading house (later known as *Casa da India* or House of India) to control spice trade. Almost a century later, the Dutch East India Company was established in 1602 to trade with India as a chartered company.

Spain, too, had a company called the Royal Barcelona Trading Company to the Indies, which operated from 1755 to 1785 and exploited the Caribbean, Puerto Rico, Santo Domingo and Margarita. And, of course, we in India know how the East India Company looted India. It was formed in London in 1600 as a joint-stock company and ended up ruling a large part of India till 1858, when the British government took direct control of the country after India's First War of Independence.

The investors in all the above as well as similarly established colonial companies had a keen interest in knowing about the colonies to make investment decisions. They needed some system, independent of company officials, to know what was happening in the countries where they operated because that would determine their profits. Thus, an entire communication system was essentially developed between the colonizers and colonies to take care of these business interests and military objectives in the occupied territories as events needed reporting from the perspective of the colonial investor, be it a company or government. From the investors' perspective, the people in the colonies were simply objects and nothing more. As such, an imperialistic outlook was an inbuilt trait in the origin of the Western media's reporting of the colonies during the eighteenth and nineteenth centuries and of the developing nations later in the twentieth and twenty-first centuries.

The reporter, in a way, followed the explorer. One can't but agree with Anthony Smith when he argues that 'reporting is exploration carried by another means. A kind of inevitability of domination is thus built Into the Western conception of the world. The globe is seen in terms of the West's need for it.'[4] The entire edifice of the Western media's reporting of the colonies was based on this need to give the relevant information to the investors or the occupiers. They were commissioned and worked for their masters. Historically, the media never came to developing societies as an independent observer to see and perceive things as they were; it came wearing pre-decided blinkers. It had specific interests, a purpose and a goal to achieve. Hence, it is safe to say that the media, developed over the centuries of colonial rule, had a pre-set agenda defined by the investors and masters to follow. It was fundamentally to help the benefactor create wealth, annex territories and spread Christianity.

---

[4]Smith, Anthony, *The Geopolitics of Information: How Western Culture Dominates the World*, Faber and Faber, London, 1980, p. 24.

COMMERCE AND EVANGELICAL PURSUITS GO HAND IN HAND

> When the Portuguese first landed in Calicut, one of the crew members of Vasco da Gama was asked what they had come for. He had replied that they had come to seek 'Christians and spices'. The answer was a succinct definition of the two things that the Portuguese had in mind—one, missionary; the other, commercial. The governor of Goa said in 1545 that the Portugese had come to India with a crucifix in one hand and a sword in the other, and the spirit of their rule seems to be typified by a figure sculptured on the viceroy arch in Goa, that of a saint whose foot is on the neck of a prostrate Indian and whose band holds a drawn sword pointing towards India.[5]

This instance cited by L.S.S. O'Malley provides a window into the commercial and evangelical intentions of Portugal. However, other Imperial powers were no exception, and the Western media worked to achieve imperial objectives. Professor John M. MacKenzie writes in the introduction to *Reporting the Raj: The British Press and India, c. 1880–1922* that imperialism and the modern press developed precisely at the same time. He states, 'The Press fed off empire voraciously and, in doing so, came to have an influence upon affairs.'[6] This is not surprising as the Empire believed that the press was an

[5]O'Malley, L.S.S., *Modern India and the West*, Oxford University Press, London, 1941, p. 44.

[6]Kaul, Chandrika, *Reporting the Raj: The British Press and India, c. 1880–1922*, Manchester University Press, Manchester, 2003, p. xii.

instrument of carrying forward the imperial legacies. Lord Curzon, chancellor of the University of Oxford and former viceroy of India, declared in 1909 that pressmen were 'Live Rails' of the Empire, connecting the outskirts with the heart. At the first Imperial Press Conference in Oxford, he boasted that the University also produced journalists besides civil servants.[7]

Journalists worked for imperial powers and none exemplifies it better than the life, works and writings of Henry Morton Stanley (1841–1904). He was born in England and migrated to the USA when he was 18. Described as a Welsh-born American journalist and explorer, he represented the *New York Herald* as a special correspondent (1867). He travelled to Africa and wrote extensively, including books like *Through the Dark Continent* (1878). Initially, Stanley wanted to go to Congo to represent British interests. He possibly wanted to establish a colony for them. But his negotiations with the British failed as he was unsuccessful in convincing the British government that he could represent its imperial interests in Africa. Then he tried his luck with King Leopold II of Belgium. King Leopold hired him privately, and Stanley established a private colony for the king in Africa. It is reported that his efforts paved the way for the creation of the Congo Free State, privately owned by Leopold. After returning from Africa, he was re-naturalized as a British citizen. He contested elections and entered British Parliament as a Member of Parliament (MP) in the Lower House (1895–1900). He was knighted in 1899 for his services to the Crown. The famous explorer-journalist once declared before the Manchester Chamber of Commerce:

[7]Ibid. 1.

> There are 50 million people beyond the gateway to Congo, and the cotton spinners of Manchester are waiting to clothe them. Birmingham foundries are glowing with the red metal that will presently be made into ironwork for them and trinkets that shall adorn dusky bosoms, and the ministers of Christ are zealous to bring them, the poor benighted heather, into the Christian fold.[8]

Stanley's is a direct example of the identities of pressmen and colonizers overlapping, demonstratively to fulfil an evangelical agenda. Another instance of the overlapping of evangelical and explorative purposes is presented in a journal entry by Columbus, written on his voyage in 1492:

> Your Highnesses, as Catholic Christians, and princess who love and promote the holy Christian faith, and are enemies of the doctrine of Mahomet, and of all idolatry and heresy, determined to send me, Christopher Columbus, to the above-mentioned countries of India, to see the said princes, people, and territories, and to learn their disposition and the proper method of converting them to our holy faith; and furthermore directed that I should not proceed by land to the East, as is customary, but by a Westerly route, in which direction we have hitherto no certain evidence that anyone has gone.[9]

---

[8]Moon, P.T., *Imperialism and World Politics*, The Macmillan Company, New York, 1926, p. 26.

[9]'Medieval Sourcebook: Christopher Columbus—Extracts from Journal', *Fordham University*, March 1996, http://tinyurl.com/y9samyf8. Accessed on 3 January 2024.

This worldview expounded by Stanley and other explorers was applauded by their European audience. Writer Chandrika Kaul describes this phenomenon as 'imperial patriotism', which was 'profitable, and imperial values were projected by such diverse means as music halls, missionary societies, Churches, book publishers, magazines and juvenile literature, school texts, cinema and organisations like the Boy Scouts'.[10]

What Stanley had said was not expressed in some ancient time but only about 150 years back. Smith argues that Stanley was a newsman and his professional integrity was beyond doubt, but 'his information was collected under the inspiration of a socially accepted doctrine of colonialism, in which the pursuit of loot, markets and the Christian faith are subsumed into a single quest which was undoubtedly emotionally uplifting for his audience in imperial England'.[11]

The explorer-reporters unabashedly wore many hats during those times. Often, the reporter and the explorer would work together towards their common goal, that is, bringing 'enlightenment' and 'progress' to these conquered, 'dark' lands. Individuals such as Stanley are eulogized in Western writings as builders of roads, railways and other infrastructure and 'modernizing' societies that the West considered primitive.

The press played the imperial game willingly. For example, in India, instructions were issued to the reporters from time to time as to how to cover events from the East. They were asked to ignore 'Murders and Outrages' of the indigenous

---

[10]Kaul, Chandrika, *Reporting the Raj: The British Press and India, c. 1880–1922*, Manchester University Press, Manchester, 2003, p. 8.

[11]Smith, Anthony, *The Geopolitics of Information: How Western Culture Dominates the World*, Faber and Faber, London, 1980, p. 25.

populations. However, the murder of even an obscure missionary always necessitated reporting.[12]

Non-Western beliefs, especially religious ones, were not only considered primitive but abhorrent, and the Western media played a major part in spreading this narrative. Stephen Prothero, for example, in an essay titled 'Hinduphobia and Hinduphila in U.S. Culture', writes that 'anti-Hindu invective was spread [...] by newspaper reporters'.[13] He says that reporting on a case in 1911 various newspapers, including the *New York Times* and *Boston Herald*, referred to Hindu rites as 'queer'. The *New York Times* called Hinduism a 'strange cult' while *Boston Herald* wrote that actual Hinduism 'was not about mystical union with God but about public prostitution, idol worship, antisocial ascetics, child brides, and the caste system'.[14]

In the same year, the *New York Times* wrote in a book review column that the Hindus were fatalistic by nature. The editors stated that 'to inculcate any modern faith it is necessary, first, to eradicate this stuporous principle'. In the review, the editors lamented that there were only a handful of missionaries in India for the spread of the Gospel.[15]

In 1956, when the GoI tried to put restrictions on proselytizing activities by foreign missionaries, the *Guardian*

---

[12]Kaul, Chandrika, *Reporting the Raj: The British Press and India, c. 1880–1922*, Manchester University Press, Manchester, 2003, p. 8.

[13]Prothero, Stephen, 'Hinduphobia and Hinduphila in U.S. Culture', *The Stranger's Religion: Fascination and Fear*, Anna Lännström (ed.), University of Notre Dame Press, Notre Dame, USA, p. 16.

[14]Ibid.

[15]'IS INDIA RIPE FOR CHRISTIANITY?; A Historian Who Believes It to Be, Since Hinduism Has Failed There,' *New York Times*, 3 September 1911, http://tinyurl.com/ejas9urz. Accessed on 3 January 2024.

wrote that missionaries in India are having a 'thin time' again. The paper lamented that nobody liked an outsider to show the way to God.[16]

There is a definite similarity in thoughts between Columbus in 1492, da Gama in 1545, H.M. Stanley in 1886, the *New York Times* in 1911 and the *Guardian* in 1956. But the question is, has it changed at all? While many like Smith argue that the West has finally realized that its acts were highly embarrassing, there is a difference between feeling embarrassed and changing one's narrative and perspective. There have been some adjustments in the Western attitude. However, the fundamentals of the narratives remain the same. The style of the arguments may have changed, but has the intent transformed? It does not seem so.

Take, for example, the issue of evangelization. As demonstrated, 'civilizing' the rest of the world by converting it to Christianity had been a fundamental theme of the West's narrative. Even today, when agencies run and funded by the US government release reports like those on freedom of religion,[17] these reports are from a Christian perspective and not from that of other religions such as Hinduism and Buddhism. Whenever the religions common in other parts of the world try to assert their identities and create a system where conversion to Christianity by allurement and other dubious means is discouraged, a hue and cry regarding the 'freedom of religion' is made.

---

[16]Zinkin, Taya, 'Christian Missionaries under Fire in India—Archive, 1956', *Guardian*, 20 July 2017, http://tinyurl.com/3hbctm26. Accessed on 3 January 2024.

[17]*International Religious Freedom Reports*, US Department of State, http://tinyurl.com/ywx7zthz. Accessed on 22 January 2024.

Since Prime Minister Narendra Modi's government came to power in India in 2014, the freedom of religion reports have been targeting India, often comparing it with Afghanistan, Saudi Arabia, Russia and Iran, etc. Take, for example, a 2015 *Newsweek* report that asked Modi to 'embrace religious tolerance'.[18] The *Time* magazine, too, filed a report in May 2023 titled 'The U.S. Just Released a Scathing Report on Religious Freedom in India'.[19]

The GoI has consistently rejected these reports and called them 'flawed, motivated and biased'. These have been described as based on 'misinformation and flawed understanding'.[20]

But the Western media invariably joins this chorus and plays up these reports, using them to target the Modi government. They routinely publicize these reports calling the Modi government a 'Hindu nationalist government'.

PREJUDICE AGAINST THE UNKNOWN

It was not surprising that the Western explorers and occupiers declared all the civilizations they 'conquered', often by dubious means, to be primitive. When they reached these lands, they had a preconceived notion of

---

[18]Curtis, Lisa, 'India: Modi Must Embrace Religious Tolerance', *Newsweek*, 3 Febraury 2015, https://tinyurl.com/yzf3y22r. Accessed on 22 January 2024.

[19]Rajvanshi, Astha, 'U.S. Releases Scathing Report on Religious Freedom in India', *Time*, 16 May 2023, tinyurl.com/4ewdsxz8. Accessed on 22 January 2024.

[20]Mohan, Geeta, 'Flawed, Motivated, Biased: Govt Rejects US Religious Freedom Report That Criticised India for "Attacks" on Minorities', *India Today*, 17 May 2023, https://tinyurl.com/22fejtsh. Accessed on 22 January 2024.

these societies and lands, as demonstrated in the previous section. In fact, an image of a primitive society already existed in the popular Western imagination, as illustrated by its literature. There are a number of *mappemonde* available in Western literature to describe other unknown civilizations. There is one such mappemonde found in a copy of Ranulf Higden's *Polychronicon.* There is one such mappemonde found in a copy of Ranulf Higden's *Polychronicon.* It enjoyed considerable popularity in the fifteenth century and was considered to be the standard work on general history. Its descriptions of peoples from other nations (heads growing beneath shoulders, umbrella lips, etc.) may have been thought of as amusing, but this kind of imagery had a deep impact on the common Western psyche. The general Western population believed these to be true.

The problem of unbalanced and distorted media coverage in the Western media is not peculiar to India alone, as is illustrated by the Suriname story. Most of the developing world is perennially a victim of these misguided priorities in news media. Roger Tatarian, a journalist of Turkish origin who worked as the vice president of United Press International (UPI), acknowledged this. There was indeed a serious issue of imbalance about how the Western agencies covered the developing world. Tatarian states:

> There is an acknowledged tendency among Western media ... to devote the greatest attention to the Third World in times of disaster, crisis and confrontation. The agencies are no less interested in disaster, crisis and confrontation when it exists in the developed world. But

their daily file of news of the developed world is vast, even when there is no crisis. The same is not true of much of the Third World.[21]

GENESIS OF INTERNATIONAL NEWS AGENCIES

With time, the gathering and dissemination of news has evolved. It became more organized than the reporter-and-explorer coterie. News agencies came into being. But the motivation, of course, remained the same, that is, preservation of the existing power structure.

Issues such as free flow of information, religious freedom and market access are understood by the Western media as a one-way street even today. The international financial structure remains heavily in favour of the developed world, and global institutions are still being controlled by the West.

Newspapers and other media organizations cannot deploy their staff in every part of the world to get coverage. Therefore, they have to depend on the agency feeds, especially for the bulk of their foreign coverage. Much of this distortion and imbalance that the Third World faces comes out of agencies' coverage. The news flow in the world is mostly controlled by four news agencies: Associated Press (AP), Reuters, Agence France-Presse (AFP) and UPI. It is important to understand the genesis, evolution, history and working of these international news agencies.

---

[21]Tatarian, Roger, 'News Flow in the Third World: An Overview', *The Third World and Press Freedom*, P.C. Horton (ed.), Praeger, New York, 1978, p. 42.

Evolution of Information Business

An enterprising Frenchman, Charles-Louis Havas, used to translate foreign newspapers and used to sell them to local businessmen, diplomats, traders, financiers, the government and the French press. He soon realized that newspapers had their own biases. Thus, he started to employ his own correspondents and founded the news agency, Havas, in 1835. Agence Havas became the first news agency in the world. It evolved services for the speedy translation of foreign newspapers, and, above all, improved Havas's communications by using the semaphore telegraph.[22] Agence Havas established the first telegraph service in France in 1845. The advent of the telegraph made it possible for clients outside France to use the agency's services. Smith states, 'So rapidly was the demand for commercial information increasing—on businesses, stocks, currencies, commodities, harvests, extractive products—in the middle of the nineteenth century, that the news business never faltered. Each political shift, every insurrection and revolution, occasioned a flurry in the money markets and the swift communications of fresh events was a most valuable service.'[23]

This information business was so lucrative and enticing that two Havas employees, Paul Reuter and Bernhard Wolff, set up their own agencies. Reuter established the Reuters News Agency in London in 1851; Wolff started his agency, Wolffs Telegraphisches Bureau (WTB), in Berlin in 1849. In the next two decades, national news agencies were set up

---

[22]*News Agencies: Their Structure and Operation,* UNESCO, Paris, 1953, https://tinyurl.com/wa263rej. Accessed on 8 December 2023.

[23]Smith, Anthony, *The Geopolitics of Information: How Western Culture Dominates the World,* Faber and Faber, London, 1980, p. 76.

in many countries of Europe catering primarily to domestic information needs.

Meanwhile, in the USA, the New York Associated Press was established as a news cooperative in 1846. A few regional cooperatives were also started in other parts of the USA. These cooperatives signed news exchange contracts with Havas, Reuters or Wolff for foreign news. One of these regional agencies, the Western Associated Press, set up a new independent company called the Associated Press. This new company concluded an exclusive contract with Reuters, which provided it with the services of Havas and Wolff and its own, which in practice gave the AP the monopoly of all European news in the USA. The AP grew rapidly and led to the demise of the formidable New York Associated Press and others.[24] It grew into what the AP is today. Many national domestic news agencies were launched in many parts of the world during the same period.

Cartelization of News

There was fierce competition to control the business of information to begin with. However, the agencies soon realized that it was very costly to collect and disseminate the information to their respective clients individually. Hence, they carved out the entire world into zones and divided it exclusively among themselves. Thus began the cartelization of news by the agencies.[25] The agency cartel formally came into being in January 1870 in a quadripartite agreement

---

[24]*News Agencies: Their Structure and Operation*, UNESCO, Paris, 1953, https://tinyurl.com/wa263rej. Accessed on 8 December 2023.
[25]Ibid.

between the three big European agencies and the New York Associated Press.[26] This agreement provided for a division of the world into several zones. Each of the agencies decided not to compete and have a monopoly over the collection and distribution of news in the designated zone.

Paris-based Havas had France, Switzerland, Italy, Spain, Portugal, and Central and South America. London-based Reuters took over the entire British Empire, Turkey and the Far East. Egypt was shared by Havas and Reuters. Germany-based WTB took control of news operations in Germany, Austria, the Netherlands, Scandinavia, Russia and the Balkans. The territory of the USA was exclusively assigned to the New York Associated Press.[27]

The four agencies, thus, secured control of news flow throughout the world. The agreement lasted for about half a century. The quadripartite agreement was almost reminiscent of imperial powers dividing their world empire for the loot and plunder. The agencies did employ the locals, but they were taken in the same way as the Company Bahadur prior to 1857 and the Crown thereafter employed Indians to serve the empire. Their training, news gathering processes, protocol, factors for prioritization of news, vocabulary, style of writing, etc., were all but standardized.

News and information is infinite to a large extent, meaning that the events, happenings and information flow are continuous. However, the resources to cover such news are always finite. Therefore, the most important decision for any news professional is what to cover and what to leave.

---

[26]Ibid.

[27]Ibid.

This is guided by the inherent interests of the promoting organization and the market for its news. The news professional in any organization is inherently trained to follow this inbuilt DNA.

It is clear to me that the Western media gathered news from the perspective of the larger interests of imperial powers. The events and personalities covered by them were mere 'subjects' chosen from the pre-decided perspective. As the media largely represented the colonial interests, subjects residing in the colonies had no say in deciding the tone and tenor of any story. News businesses used these subjects not as live participants but basically a material for making a product created for a separate market. The market comprised largely of colonizing countries. It was contextualized only for the market served and not from the perspective of the 'subject' in the story or where it was happening.

News was made into an exchangeable commodity by a cartel created by international agencies. Smith, in his book, says that the agencies played a crucial role in advancing international microsystems to promote capitalism. According to him, Reuter built his Eastern empire on the cotton trade. He used to supply important data to British merchants regarding cotton cultivation in India and other countries of the East. He also provided political information on China to his clients. These were very valuable inputs to the investors and the political class. In this process, Reuter created a network of people in South Asia who collected information on his behalf. This resulted in laying the foundation of the Indian press industry. He not only built telegraph lines in his exclusive zone but was even contracted to build a railway line from the Caspian to the Persian Gulf with branch lines.[28] Thus, he leveraged the media network to build other businesses.

Emergence of National News Agencies

The quadrilateral agreement among the world news agencies collapsed after World War I. In the meantime, as countries better understood the importance of news and information flow for creating and furthering the political narratives, almost each country started to have its own news agency. This began with the continents of Europe and North America in the late nineteenth and early twentieth centuries.

As stated previously, division of the world by the news agencies was similar to this geopolitical power balance among the imperialist powers. This balance was disturbed with the advent of a new force in Europe when the Bolsheviks came to power in Russia. It was soon reflected in the news and information structures in Europe to begin with, and it later spread to other parts of the globe. As the process of decolonization gathered pace after World War II, various news agencies were formed in countries across the continents of Asia, Africa and Latin America. For example, the Press Trust of India (PTI) was founded in India in 1947.

However, the national news agencies focussed on events in a particular geography. For international events and happenings, they had arrangements with the international agencies. It must be mentioned that many of the national agencies posted their correspondents in other countries as per domestic requirements and larger geopolitical interests

---

[28]Smith, Anthony, *The Geopolitics of Information: How Western Culture Dominates the World*, Faber and Faber, London, 1980, pp. 78–9.

of the country. They continue to do so even today. However, the news covered by these correspondents remains limited in scope and scale.

Countries have tried to create alternatives for the Big Four from time to time. For example, Telegrafnoye Agentstvo Sovetskogo Soyuza (TASS) was founded in 1904 in Russia.[29] After the communists took control, it was called Rossijskoj Telegrafnoie Agenburo or the Telegraph Agency of the Soviet Union.[30] The agency was an important contributor of news flow for the socialist bloc countries during the Cold War era. However, with the demise of the Soviet Union, its contribution declined. Xinhua has been trying to create an alternate model based on Chinese Communist Party ideology.

Even though national news agencies were founded in various countries, the influence of the big international agencies did not decline. The national news agencies continued to remain dependent on these agencies for world news. An analysis of three international crises in the 1960s showed that 87 per cent of coverage in four Norwegian newspapers came from the four agencies.[31] A monthly study was done on the most important papers circulating in India, Kenya, Lebanon, Japan and Norway during 1961 and 1968.[32] The results showed that at least 50 per cent of news items were sourced from the same four big agencies. In 1977, a

---

[29]*News Agencies Their Structure and Operation*, UNESCO, Paris, 1953, https://tinyurl.com/wa263rej. Accessed on 8 December 2023.

[30]Krasnoboka, Natalya, 'Russia', *European Journalism Centre*, http://tinyurl.com/2x4bf4et. Accessed on 15 December 2023.

[31]Mowlana, H., *International Flow of Information: A Global Report and Analysis*, UNESCO, Paris, 1985, p. 23.

[32]Ibid.

study of international news coverage was conducted in 14 Asian newspapers.[33] The analysis proved that over three-quarters of non-local Third-World news came from the four agencies. The trend was the same even in the developed world. Around 70 per cent of American news in Canadian newspapers was provided by the same agencies in 1978.[34] Journalist Fernando Reyes Matta's analysis of 16 dailies revealed the same pattern in 14 Latin American nations. It was discovered that 80 per cent of international news came from the big four.[35]

As these agencies are part of the market-driven Western ecosystem, two factors have a critical impact on their decision-making and prioritization process. One is the market and the other is the international power equilibrium. Many believe that the agencies cannot survive on their own if not supported directly or indirectly by a government. A committee of experts in India said it in so many words in its report:

> Historically speaking, the existing world news agencies have been able to develop only in the context of direct or indirect state support. Reuters was established and grew when Britain was the world's foremost power. Its services were automatically subscribed to by newspapers in countries which were ruled by Britain. AFP also developed when France was an imperial power, and indeed the French Government participated in the share capital and in the board of management of AFP till about

[33]Ibid.

[34]Ibid.

[35]Ibid.

> a decade ago. The great economic influence of the USA not only in the Americas but also overseas has had little to do with the development of the two agencies, AP and UPI.[36]

The explosion of social media and the advent of user-generated content (UGC) have created a ripple in the established news and information ecosystem. However, the grip of the well-entrenched players in the information business—agencies, newspapers, TV and other traditional news establishments—on the overall narrative building is still very strong. The news agencies still control the bulk of third-party information flow in the world. Their priorities are still largely driven by the existing power balance in the world which is heavily tilted in the Western world's favour. The digital and social media seem to have democratized content generation, dissemination and flow. But this is only partly true. The fact is that this new-age information ecosystem is more tightly controlled by the West. A few for-profit companies based in the USA have an almost absolute monopoly on digital and social assets. The developing world lacks financial and technological resources to combat the tsunami of increased information flow that is impacting their social, political and cultural fabric more deeply than ever. Led by complex algorithms, machine intelligence and sophisticated artificial intelligence (AI) tools, narrative building has become more lopsided. Never in human history has news dissemination been so controlled and centralized in the hands of a few as it is today. The NWIO still remains an elusive dream for the developing countries of the Global South.

---

[36]*Report of the Committee on News Agencies*, Ministry of Information and Broadcasting, Government of India, New Delhi, 1977, p. 54.

Chapter 2

WESTERN MEDIA IN POST-INDEPENDENCE INDIA

After the end of World War II, newly independent countries wanted to have their own national agencies rather than depend on Western news agencies, which largely looked at world events from the West's point of view. Thus, in India, the PTI came into being in 1947. A year later, in September 1948, Reuters entered into an agreement with it, whereby areas from Cairo to Singapore were assigned exclusively to the PTI to cover and send news.[1] Earlier, this was done by a subsidiary of Reuters called the Associate Press of India.

REUTERS SERVES BRITISH INTERESTS

The collaboration between the PTI and Reuters was not very smooth. The fundamental difference between them was how

[1]*News Agencies: Their Structure and Operation*, UNESCO, Paris, 1953, https://tinyurl.com/wa263rej. Accessed on 8 December 2023.

journalists from both agencies looked at international issues. While Reuters's despatches came with the perspective and geopolitical interest of the West, the PTI correspondents' reporting was not in line with how Reuters wanted to see certain issues.[2] Thus, the latter ended up posting British staffers in Pakistan.[3] This move by Reuters was against the agreement it had signed with the PTI and caused differences between the two agencies, which turned so bitter that Reuters asked to renegotiate the agreement.

In 1952, the chairman of the PTI, Kasturi Srinivasan, asked PM Nehru to help resolve the dispute between the two media agencies. In his response, in a letter dated 19 August 1952, PM Nehru stated that he was very reluctant to interfere in the partnership arrangements between two news agencies and that it was the responsibility of the PTI board to smoothen things. However, he went on to point out that 'undoubtedly, Reuters has represented in the past, and largely represents today, the British background. They have every right to do so. I do not object to that. But I do not see why our background and policy should be subordinated to the British background and policy.'[4]

When the PTI–Reuters contract was about to be renewed in 1953, the latter wanted to add a few provisions that would have curtailed the PTI's editorial freedom, according to Nehru.[5] Had the provisions been incorporated, it would have given Reuters an upper hand in all important editorial

---

[2]S. Gopal (ed.), *Selected Works of Jawaharlal Nehru,* Volume 19, Second Series, Jawaharlal Nehru Memorial Fund, New Delhi, p. 179.

[3]Ibid. 180.

[4]Ibid. 181.

[5]Ibid. 181–2.

matters. However, the Indian leadership rightly believed that India could not afford to have the wrong international image and stance portrayed by the dominant Western media, particularly the English media. An example of this discrepancy is how a British Reuters correspondent reported that a statue of Gandhi in Karachi had fallen in a gale, when it was actually vandalized by miscreants.[6] Reuters resisted the Indian point of view in this coverage of news. When the PTI desk in its London office decided to check the story from its own correspondent in Karachi, it found the narration incorrect.[7] The story was subsequently changed by the PTI editors posted in London. However, this affirmation of freedom of expression and editorial autonomy by the PTI desk in London did not sit well with Reuters. According to PM Nehru, the Reuters management wanted the PTI to be kept in a 'subordinate position'[8] and that the blooming of the PTI into a national and independent news agency didn't suit Reuters's larger interests.

Another example of the discrepancy in focus of news covered by the PTI and Reuters includes that of the Korean peninsula crisis, wherein Reuters's coverage addressed the Communist Chinese forces as 'aggressors', which went against the Indian foreign policy of the time.[9] Moreover, reports by Reuters from the United Nations (UN) also lacked a focus on Indian perspective that the domestic newspapers needed. For example, the Reuters correspondents reporting from the UN would cover the speeches by British representatives in detail,

---

[6]Ibid. 179–80.

[7]Ibid.

[8]Ibid.

[9]Ibid.

but speeches by Indian and other countries' representatives would be dismissed in a single line.[10] India's point of view on international issues, particularly on matters related to Eastern Europe, was never given coverage in such stories either. Whenever such stories were filed by the agency, the PTI desk had to remind the Reuters editors that the Indian newspapers would like to know the perspective of the Indian leadership on issues concerning the other side of the Iron Curtain. However, the Reuters editorial staff, which had an anti-communism stance, would simply ignore such requests.[11]

Theoretically, Reuters claimed to disseminate 'truthful and unbiased news.'[12] However, PM Nehru was convinced that it was more of a facade than reality. He did not believe that any news agency in the world was free of government control or completely unbiased. He said that even if there was no deliberate distortion, the policies and background of the country are reflected in the reports of the agency depending on its location. He also believed that more often than not, the PTI would have to 'surrender' to Reuters.[13]

Prime Minister Nehru was indeed right in his analysis of the working of the Western media. While it does take a position against and criticizes the regimes in the West, it never goes against the larger interests of the Western bloc. It is not true only of newspapers and news agencies back then; even today, in the days of the digital and social media explosion, the big Western media outfits and digital and social media platforms function in a similar fashion. Their

[10]Ibid.
[11]Ibid. 180.
[12]Ibid. 182.
[13]Ibid. 181.

DNA is the same. The digital giants—Google, Facebook and X (formerly Twitter), among others—seem to follow in the same footsteps.

The conclusion of the PTI–Reuters tension was that the former decided not to go ahead with the changes proposed by the Reuters board, and the partnership arrangement between the two agencies lapsed. The PTI–Reuters incident illustrates that though the Empire was forced to give political freedom to its dominions, it never wanted to give away its information hegemony.

BRITISH PRESS USES HYDERABAD TO DENIGRATE SARDAR PATEL

On 15 September 1948, two days before the signing of the instrument of accession by the Nizam of Hyderabad, British Parliament decided to discuss the situation in Hyderabad.[14] The Opposition leader Anthony Eden, quoting some newspaper reports in the House of Commons, asked the government to strongly take up the issue and intervene in what he called the 'invasion of Hyderabad' in the UN Security Council (UNSC) meeting to be held the next day in Paris.[15] He also urged the British foreign secretary to confirm if the newspaper report was correct. In reply, the British foreign secretary said that a war-like situation has emerged in Hyderabad. He also said that the situation was likely to go out of control if Britain did not

[14]'Debate on the Address: Volume 456—Debated on Wednesday 15 September 1948', *UK Parliament*, http://tinyurl.com/2zzmw4fj. Accessed on 15 December 2023.

[15]Ibid. Column 79.

intervene and that it could spread to other areas.[16]

There were more consequences that followed the British press reports on Hyderabad. What was depicted by the media resulted in an altogether different perception of the situation in India for a section of the British population. Consequently, Gordon Collyer, a common UK citizen, following the press reports about Hyderabad and Sardar Patel's actions and after discussion of the issue in the House of Commons, wrote a letter to Patel. In his letter, he expressed his unhappiness over Patel objecting to Britain's discussion of Indian affairs in British Parliament. He was perturbed with what he had read in British papers about the situation in Hyderabad as well as by the way Patel talked. In his letter dated 7 October 1948, he wrote that he was a commoner and it was a letter from a nobody to somebody. He said that he was writing on behalf of common British citizens, and that thousands like him disapprove of Patel's speeches. Condemning the way Patel took actions in Hyderabad, he said that 'internationality' was more important than Indian sovereignty.[17]

In his reply to Collyer, dated 13 October 1948, Patel said that he has been misunderstood and that his speeches have been misreported by the British press. He added that the reasons for this disconnect were steeped in both the immediate and distant past. Patel also took a strong stance against the criticism of Indian actions in British Parliament. He questioned why issues of Hyderabad and Kashmir were

[16]'Orders of the Day: Volume 456—Debated on Wednesday 15 September 1948', *UK Parliament*, http://tinyurl.com/2bjc7a5w. Accessed on 15 December 2023.

[17]Das, Durga (ed.), *Sardar Patel's Correspondence, 1945–50*, Volume 6, Navajivan Publishing House, Ahmedabad, 1973, pp. 454–5.

allowed to be discussed in British Parliament when matters of no other dominion were debated. 'Have you, for instance, debated Ireland?' he asked rhetorically. He posed the denial of fundamental rights to Indians and Africans by the Europeans in South Africa as a more urgent issue and argued that this was never discussed in British Parliament.[18]

Patel made it very clear in his letter that he had an unflinching commitment to the freedom of expression, especially that of the press. However, he added that no criticism had the right to malign the domestic autonomy of nations, Commonwealth nations in particular. He further wrote that the British press was responsible for creating a deliberately misrepresented image of India for the British public.[19]

∽

In India, the integration of Hyderabad was seen as a successful endeavour undertaken by Sardar Patel, who had convinced more than 560 princely states[20] to join independent India. He was regarded as a hero who was instrumental in uniting India. However, the British media built a narrative that the Indian government had not followed the agreement that the Queen's government had entered with the princely states, especially Hyderabad. It also downplayed the violence unleashed by *razakars* led by Nizam Kasim Razvi, who was said to have recruited 'a force numbering

---

[18]Ibid. 455–6.

[19]Ibid.

[20]'Accession Integration Unification', *Sardar Patel: The Man Who United India*, http://tinyurl.com/2r5v3uuf. Accessed on 15 December 2023.

anywhere between 50,000 to 2 lakh men.'[21] He had wanted to establish Hyderabad as an Islamic state. A wave of violence and terror was unleashed by these militiamen recruited by Razvi.[22]

UK *takes* Hyderabad Issue to UNSC

The UK government cleverly secured parliamentary sanction to take the internal issue of India to the UNSC on the basis of newspaper reports. This is how the British media ecosystem worked to undermine India's interests. A UK newspaper published a one-sided account of what was happening in Hyderabad, which was brought up in Parliament and the issue was then taken to the UNSC, which was being chaired by the UK. The sheer presumption and self-importance is astonishing.

It is also very interesting to note that the question of widespread violence in the then newly independent Burma (now Myanmar) also came up in the same discussion in British Parliament. However, while the House of Commons encouraged a debate on India, the UK's official line in Burma's case was of non-interference. The British government maintained that the violence was to be handled by the new government in Burma. In the same debate, Ernest Bevin, Secretary of State for Foreign Affairs, expressed his sympathies with the new government in Burma and offered to help restore order in the country only if the Burmese government

---

[21]Devulapalli, Rahul, 'Tracing Razakar Legacy: When Razvi's Granddaughter Visited Hyderabad', *The Week*, 30 September 2021, http://tinyurl.com/34rawa5x. Accessed on 3 January 2024.

[22]Shastri, Rahul A., 'The Hyderabad Liberation Day', *Samvit Kendra*, 17 September 2016, http://tinyurl.com/nfupvffn. Accessed on 3 January 2024.

required. Otherwise, he said that it was to be handled by Burma. He praised the way the Burmese government was dealing with the situation and hoped that it would soon be able to find a solution to the crisis.[23]

The situations in both Burma and India were almost similar. Both had become independent in a similar time frame and both were facing internal issues. However, the British decided to intervene in the case of India, while choosing to look the other way in the case of Burma. I do not think they ever believed that India was a single entity. This is in complete contrast to what most of India has believed over the centuries. India has been seen as one nation despite different rulers controlling different geographies. From ancient times, different kings and rulers have been perceived as separate administrative units, not separate nations. India has been seen as a whole both by outsiders and insiders. Hence, the country's division between princely states and British India before Independence was merely a question of who administered what areas as far as the people of India were concerned. Therefore, when the question of amalgamation of these separate units came, Patel emphasized this inherent oneness of India, and his insistence had an emotional impact. That is why almost all princely states, except a couple, signed an instrument of accession and chose to merge with the nation.

While there will always be differences, fault lines and issues in a large country like India, the British government and the dominant English media tried to create a negative narrative

---

[23]'Orders of the Day: Volume 456—Debated on Wednesday 15 September 1948', *UK Parliament*, http://tinyurl.com/2bjc7a5w. Accessed on 15 December 2023.

in order for these differences to become unmanageable. The British could not fathom the thought that Sardar Patel had been successful in integrating the princely states with such alacrity.

WHEN GANDHI GOT UPSET WITH THE ENGLISH PRESS

Gandhi was generally not known to show his anger, at least not in public. But on 9 December 1947, things were different. He was livid with the canard spread in the press about him and Sardar Patel going to Pilani from Delhi for a 'change of air'. On that day, he started his prayer meeting speech by criticizing the rumour mongering by the newspapers. He was angrier because after the newspaper reports were published, the AP had sent him a query asking him if the rumours were true.

Remember, these were the days soon after Partition, when the communal frenzy was at its peak. Lakhs of Indians were subjected to barbaric loot, rape, kidnapping and murder as a result of the ill-conceived, hurried and unnatural drawing of the boundary line in the heart of Punjab and Bengal by Sir Cyril Radcliffe, a retired UK barrister who had never travelled to India and had almost no idea of India's history, legacy and people.

Gandhi, at the time, was visiting the trouble-torn areas in the country and, on 9 December, was camping in Delhi. He visited areas in the city to see if the suffering had lessened. The situation had remained grim with each passing day, and many thought that the two-nation theory and the creation of Pakistan on communal lines were largely to blame for the state of things at that point. Even Gandhi said in so many words,

'In my view, Pakistan is responsible for spreading this poison.'[24]

On the other hand, Sardar Patel was busy with the mammoth tasks of amalgamating the princely states and maintaining law and order in the country as the deputy PM and first home minister of India. As a part of these tasks, Patel was occupied with convincing the princely states to join India. Only Kashmir, Junagadh and Hyderabad had not signed the instrument of accession at that point. While Junagarh and Hyderabad were integrated into India through decisive action taken by Sardar Patel, Pakistan tried to take Jammu and Kashmir by force, despite Raja Hari Singh signing the instrument of accession. At this critical juncture of the country's suffering from the consequences of Partition, Gandhi and Patel could not have thought of leaving Delhi.

It will never be known exactly how the rumours of Gandhi and Patel leaving Delhi for a sojourn to Rajasthan's picturesque town of Pilani during that difficult period started. The rumours also stated that extensive arrangements had been made for their stay, so much so that truckloads of things were being brought from Jaipur to Pilani for them to have a comfortable stay, resulting in a scarcity of things in a part of Rajasthan. It was said that sugar, wheat and other provisions, sent from other cities, were among the scarce items, and that the directive for this action had come from Jaipur. Gandhi himself expressed amusement and asked that since the arrangements were for only two people, why were provisions supplied in quantities huge enough to cause scarcity? It could only mean that a large number of servants and other staff were supposed to be travelling with them. He

---

[24]*The Collected Works of Mahatma Gandhi*, Volume XC, Navajivan Trust, Ahmedabad, 1989, p. 194.

was aghast at such canard and said that he lived a simple life and that the rumours were not true.[25]

∽

One may wonder what the English media's interest in creating the rumour about Gandhi and Patel's sojourn to Pilani was. Was there any public interest involved in this? [26]

This may seem innocuous to some, and some may say that the public had been interested in knowing what Gandhi and Patel had been up to. The argument could be extended as well—the lives of public figures should be open books, and, thus, there is no harm in knowing if they were going to Pilani to take some rest. All this makes the issue look very simple.

However, narrative building starts with small stories. These small stories are created to make or break images of individuals, institutions and nations. They may seem harmless if seen in isolation, but these small pieces of information and misinformation create a lasting impact in a larger and broader context. The human mind relates more to such smaller, real-life information rather than abstract information and big stories about leaders and personalities. When one constantly feeds the mind with these fictional news stories, they take the shape of reality in a corner of the mind.

One can understand the compulsion of some tabloid-like local newspapers to indulge in this kind of gossip journalism and rumour mongering to some extent. But what about established institutions and agencies like the AP, as in this instance?

---

[25]Ibid. 200.

[26]Ibid.

Let's understand why a reporter sends a query, to begin with. Normally, when a scribe is sure of a story and wants confirmation, they send a query. They want to have their bases covered if someone questions the story later. Experience tells us that these queries are more often tools to legitimize a piece of supposed news than to dig for actual truth. The fact that a reporter had decided to send a telegram with a query about Gandhi and Patel's schedule underscores that they prima facie believed there was some truth in the gossip. If the AP really believed that it was only a rumour, it could have simply ignored it and not bothered to send a telegram to Gandhi.

Generally speaking, these queries are like double-edged swords for the recipients, and multiple outcomes work for the questioner. If the reporter doesn't get a reply in the time frame very craftily stipulated by them, the report is filed saying that no reply was received. Non-receipt of a reply in the time frame unilaterally decided by the reporter is deemed sufficient to assume that the story is true. A passive reader has no means to go into the details of why the query was not responded to in the time frame given by the reporter. Someone might have simply not received the query; some might be travelling or busy otherwise. Even when the subject denies the rumour, the reporter can say that the subject has denied it but it is believed to be true by known or unknown sources. We see such reports routinely in newspapers quoting 'highly placed sources', 'persons in the know of things', etc. So, in either case, the rumours may be posed as some kind of truth. This is a very effective tool for perception-building games. Social media enables it even more, as such information spreads like wildfires.

DR AMBEDKAR MISQUOTED BY THE ENGLISH PRESS

Gandhi and Patel were not the only leaders targeted during the early days of Independence by the English press. Almost the entire leadership of India was victim to this vilification campaign. Another important minister in the Nehru Cabinet, Dr Bhimrao Ramji Ambedkar, was also at the receiving end of misreporting by the media. Dr Ambedkar complained of the dubious role of the media in a letter to Nehru and Patel. He wrote, 'The press has never been kind to me. It has always done its best to twist facts and phrases, take them out of their context and pervert the sense of anything I have said. I fear this is what has happened to my speech at Lucknow.'[27]

The controversy, which resulted in a bitter feud between PM Nehru and Dr Ambedkar, pertains to a speech made by the latter at the Lucknow conference of the Scheduled Castes Federation on 25 April 1948. He called upon the Scheduled Castes to be more politically united so that they could exert pressure for what he considered their legitimate political rights. His speech was misreported, and it was portrayed in the press as him plotting against the government in general, and PM Nehru in particular, which was against the principle of the Cabinet's collective responsibility. Dr Ambedkar asking his supporters to be united so that they could bargain better

---

[27]Das, Durga (ed.), *Sardar Patel's Correspondence, 1945–50*, Volume 6, Navajivan Publishing House, Ahmedabad, 1973, p. 333.

in power sharing was construed as if he had gone against the collective responsibility. In this case, the reporting was done by the Indian English media, not the foreign media. However, the Indian English media was also influenced by the narrative built by the foreign agencies, especially in the initial years after Independence.

To start with, here is some background of the situation. When the first Cabinet of independent India was formed after 15 August 1947, some parties apart from the Congress were also represented in the Cabinet. Dr Shyama Prasad Mookerjee, who was made the minister of industries and supplies, was from the Hindu Mahasabha; Dr Ambedkar, who was sworn in as the law minister, was from the Scheduled Castes Federation; and Sardar Baldev Singh, who took oath as the defence minister, was from the Panthik Party, representing Sikhs. It needs to be understood that these stalwarts were not from the Congress and represented different ideologies and viewpoints. Any unnecessary friction between them and the Congress was an added burden on the stability of the newly formed government.

When the media covered Dr Ambedkar's speech, PM Nehru was influenced by the press reports and, as a result, wrote a strong letter to him. His letter dated 27 April 1948 described Dr Ambedkar's speech as going against the Congress party. He wrote that Dr Ambedkar had spoken against the PM and the deputy PM. He also asserted that if ministers speak like in that manner, then 'there is no Cabinet responsibility left.'[28]

Dr Ambedkar, in turn, responded with a detailed

[28]Ibid. 328–9.

explanation. He marked copies of his correspondence to Sardar Vallabhbhai Patel, who was then the deputy PM of India. This correspondence is very informative and makes it amply clear that the media was trying to create mischief here. The British narrative of Indians not being capable of managing their affairs was fully displayed in this instance as well.

Speaking about the Scheduled Castes Federation joining the Congress, Dr Ambedkar had told his followers that they should decide whether they should join the Congress or socialists. His advice was that they should form a separate party of scheduled castes. This third political party would be able to bargain better and hold the power balance. He had said that if they join any political party, they would only get political office but not get any real power. Dr Ambedkar wrote that with adult suffrage it was possible for scheduled castes to become a dominant political force. They just needed to be organized. They could capture political power. He added that the Congress will not remain in power forever. Even the government led by Nehru and Patel could lose elections in a democracy.[29] In a nutshell, Dr Ambedkar was talking to his supporters and asking them to be more organized and work closely with other backward classes to gain more political power, ensuring that they were not ignored in any power-sharing arrangements. One may agree or disagree with it; however, it was a legitimate political argument given by a leader to his supporters and followers. The press reported it to look like he was plotting to throw the Nehru government, from the inside. Remember, it was

[29]Ibid. 333.

the first government after Independence. Things were fluid and hence Nehru got unnerved after seeing Dr Ambedkar's speech in newspapers. Dr Ambedkar argued in his letter to Nehru that it was not true that he was attempting to turn him and Patel out of office. He said that if Nehru read his original speech, he would understand that it was not the case. He stated that he referred to Nehru and Patel in his speech in very general terms, and that it was not a political plot. He added that there was no hint of any personal ambition in his speech and his address related to future elections under the new constitution. He made it clear that he did not refer to the present government.[30] Prime Minister Nehru and Patel understood the game the media had played and the controversy ended with a letter from Sardar Patel to Dr Ambedkar.[31] Patel wrote back that he was shocked at the reported version of his speech and was relieved after receiving a letter from Dr Ambedkar. He said that he did not initially believe it when he saw the newspaper reports and thought something was not right. The controversy ended with this letter.

THE PRESS PAINTING INDIAN LEADERS IN POOR LIGHT

The whole purpose of bringing these episodes to light here is to illustrate how, in the early years of Independence, the English press was trying to prove the long-held belief of a large section of British establishment—that India was

[30]Ibid. 334.

[31]Ibid. 333.

chaotic and its leaders would never be able to handle their differences in a mature and civilized manner. Leaders like Winston Churchill believed that democracy was not meant for India. Churchill has said that India was never to be given even dominion status. He, along with a large section of the British population, held this belief from the day Gandhi was invited by Lord Irwin to London for the Round Table Conference in London. Churchill called the Indian leaders 'unpractised, unproved, unrepresentative and self-chosen'. [32]

Thanks to these erroneous notions planted in the British minds by its leaders, the prejudiced reporting in the media was widespread. The conservatives led by Churchill believed that they had brought India out of the darkness, and if they left, it would go back to the Middle Ages again.

In his speech titled 'Our Duty in India', Churchill claimed that order was established in India by a few thousand British officials. He, like many in Britain, believed that whatever progress India witnessed was because of the English rule.

> Here you have nearly three hundred and fifty million people, lifted to civilisation and to a level of peace, order, sanitation and progress far above anything they could have achieved themselves or maintain. This wonderful fact is due to the guidance and authority of a few thousand British officials responsible to Parliament who have for generations presided over the development of India.
>
> If that authority is injured or destroyed, the whole efficiency of the services, defensive, administrative,

[32]'Our Duty in India', *International Churchill Society*, http://tinyurl.com/4cbfxbfv. Accessed on 15 December 2023.

> medical, hygienic, judicial, railway, irrigation, public works and famine prevention, upon which the Indian masses depend for their culture and progress, will perish with it.[33]

These statements are indicative of a thought process that is colonial, regressive and racist to the core. They dehumanize an ancient civilization that the British subjugated through deceit and brute force. In all the years of British colonialism, whatever administrative steps the Raj had taken had only been for self-preservation and perpetuation of colonial rule. However, the idea of 'civilizing the native'—'the White Man's Burden'[34]—is ridiculous.

Before colonialism, India had an evolved consciousness and thinking—a thinking that percolated to the grassroots. For example, Indian democracy, as some believe, has flourished not because of the British 'civilizing' India but because of the eternal civilizational ethos of India's heritage, which is essentially pluralistic, non-conformist and gives space to each individual. It comes from the long-held belief of '*ekam sat viprā bahudhā vadanti*,'[35] which translates to 'Truth is one; however, wise people interpret it differently.' It can also be understood as 'The goal is one, but there are many ways to reach the destination.' Each way to reach the destination is fine. None are superior or inferior to the others. This acceptance of plurality is the very essence of Hindu civilization. The Western mindset possibly doesn't understand this complex

---

[33]Ibid.

[34]Kipling, Rudyard, 'The White Man's Burden,' *The Kipling Society*, 1899, http://tinyurl.com/bde3w9bp. Accessed on 15 December 2023.

[35]Rig Veda 1:164:46

Indian thought process and mistakes the plurality of thoughts and practices as divisive. The British, while in power, played on this and cemented these differences as divisions through their well-thought-out divisionary policies.

WHY WAS THE WEST SOFT TOWARDS PAKISTAN?

As the PTI–Reuters episode demonstrated, India did not follow the line so far as the West's foreign policy issues were concerned. This not only led to friction between two news agencies but between governments as well. The post-War world power equilibrium also came into play here. With the decisive victory of Allied Powers over Axis Powers, the international order entered another kind of war—the Cold War between the democratic countries led by the US and the socialist bloc led by the then Union of Soviet Socialist Republics (USSR). Countries in Europe, Asia, Africa and the Americas were asked to take sides. Many newly independent countries, including India, were reluctant to do so, resulting in the emergence of the NAM, of which India was a prominent member. Most of these nations had a history of being dominated by the Empire, so the NAM naturally leaned more towards the socialist bloc. The Western bloc did not like India joining the NAM, to say the least. It led to a media narrative that was not conducive to India's interests. India was considered one of the leading nations of the NAM, and, hence, it was at the receiving end of the Western bloc's policies and the attack of the Western press.

Pakistan, on the other hand, decided to join the US-led camp as a close ally. Therefore, it became a darling of the West's leadership and media. This narrative was a direct outcome of geopolitics and power balance after World War II. The dominant English media played a crucial role in shaping this anti-India narrative, and the Western news agencies, being the main disseminator of news and information, were at the forefront of this power game.

Suffice it to say, India and its leadership were at the receiving end of an information war soon after Independence. The mainstream Western media started painting India and its leadership in a particular manner, as it did not see eye-to-eye with the West on various issues. The same media was more benevolent to Pakistan and treated its leadership with kid gloves because it had decided to jump into the US-led Western camp right from the beginning. Despite being a sham democracy, Pakistan received millions of dollars of aid and good press while the Indian democracy was often castigated and ridiculed.

The media reports were used as pressure tactics in a sense. There was a definite pattern of pressurizing India and the leadership. The media would report Indian events in a particular manner, and the same would then be used to start a discussion at an international level, such as the Hyderabad issue. The well-oiled ecosystem of academic circles, NGOs, international institutions and non-government think tanks, among others, would take it up further. These debates would become media stories by themselves. A slew of stories would appear in the media based on opinions of experts from the ecosystem, and these would be presented as a fait accompli to put pressure on India diplomatically and by other means. This well-orchestrated circus was used to create a narrative on any issue. It continues even today.

Chapter 3

INDIRA OR ATAL, DOESN'T MATTER

In 1970, Pakistan was engulfed in a fierce civil war. The human rights situation in East Pakistan (presently Bangladesh) was extremely precarious. The reason for this war was the denial of political rights to the East Pakistani Bengalis by the Pakistan Army, which mostly consisted of Punjabis from West Pakistan. The issue was triggered when general elections were held in Pakistan that year for the first time after Independence in 1947. The Awami League, led by Sheikh Mujibur Rahman, won a majority both in East Pakistan and the National Assembly. However, it was unthinkable for the powerful army generals that a Bengali from the eastern part of Pakistan would be the PM. It is also significant that the geographical distance between East and West Pakistan was more than 2,000 km. In the light of this, Sheikh Mujibur was not allowed to form the government by General Yahya Khan, the then president of Pakistan.

The army tried to throttle political protests with a heavy hand. General Tikka Khan, who headed the Pakistan Army in the eastern province, launched Operation Searchlight in March 1971 to quell these widespread protests. Mukti Bahini, literally 'liberation forces', was formed by the people led by Sheikh Mujibur to fight during what we know today as the Bangladesh Liberation War. India too helped the people of East Pakistan. An estimated 1–3 million Bengalis, mostly Hindus, were killed in the military crackdown that continued for months.[1] Bangladesh officially claims that about 4 lakh Bengali women were raped by Pakistan Army and its collaborators during this period.[2] Pakistan's repression led to a humanitarian crisis of humongous proportions. The genocide in East Pakistan has been described as 'a Holocaust unmatched since Hitler'.[3] As India shared a 4,000-km border with East Pakistan, sympathizers of Sheikh Mujibur fled in lakhs to India to save their lives. Thus, India opened its borders. Refugee camps were opened in the border-states to accommodate the fleeing East Pakistani population. It was estimated that close to 10 million East Pakistanis entered the eastern states of India.[4]

At that time, the already fragile Indian economy was not able to cope with the extra burden—India was too weak

---

[1] 'The World: East Pakistan: Even the Skies Weep', *Time*, 25 October 1971, https://tinyurl.com/3trnbmu9. Accessed on 24 October 2023.

[2] Ahmed, Imtiaz, *Recognising the 1971 Bangladesh Genocide: An Appeal for Rendering Justice*, Public Diplomacy Wing, Ministry of Foreign Affairs, Government of the Peoples Republic of Bangladesh, Dhaka, 2022, https://tinyurl.com/39rysptt. Accessed on 24 October 2023.

[3] 'Looking Back at 50 Years of Bangladesh Liberation and Indo-Pakistan War of 1971', *Outlook*, 15 December 2021, http://tinyurl.com/45fbkdk5. Accessed on 3 January 2024.

[4] 'The World: East Pakistan: Even the Skies Weep', *Time*, 25 October 1971, https://tinyurl.com/3trnbmu9. Accessed on 24 October 2023.

to support these extra people. This ultimately led to a war between India and Pakistan in December 1971, in which Pakistan was conclusively defeated. Ultimately, a separate nation called Bangladesh was formed on 16 December 1971, and India was the first country to recognize it as a separate and independent state.[5]

However, in November that year, before the resolution of the situation, Indira Gandhi had gone to Washington, D.C., to brief the US leadership about the fast-deteriorating situation in East Pakistan.

WESTERN MEDIA AND INDIRA GANDHI

In the early morning of 5 November 1971 in Washington, D.C., a very short, nine-minute private meeting was convened to prepare for a summit later in the day. One of the participants in the summit was to be the visiting Indian PM Indira Gandhi. In the preparatory meeting, then US President Richard Nixon, his assistant for national security affairs Henry Kissinger and the President's assistant H.R. Haldeman were present. It started with President Nixon calling PM Indira a b***h and Kissinger chipping in, saying, 'Well, the Indians are b******s anyway.'[6]

These slurs do not appear to be hurled in any rage

---

[5] *India–Bangladesh Relations*, Ministry of External Affairs, Government of India, https://tinyurl.com/3635n5up. Accessed on 11 December 2023.

[6] '150. Conversation Among President Nixon, the President's Assistant for National Security Affairs (Kissinger), and the President's Assistant (Haldeman)', Foreign Relations of the United States, 1969–1976, Volume E–7, Documents on South Asia, 1969–1972, Office of the Historian, Foreign Service Institute, United States Department of State, https://tinyurl.com/yc26d2vj. Accessed on 11 December 2023.

or anger or in the heat of the moment but in a normal, conversational tone. The participants in the conversations seem to have said what they actually felt. In this short conversation, these demeaning and outrageous abuses were repeated a number of times.

The purpose here is not to find answers to why the top US leadership used abusive language towards India and its leadership—this prejudicial attitude of the American establishment is a subject of a deeper study. The objective here is to understand the Western media's reaction to this incident. This official conversation was declassified on 28 June 2005 when the US Bureau of Public Affairs issued a formal press release.[7]

Libel and Western Media

In journalism, it is a common practice to file stories immediately when any such information becomes public. In this case, the information did not arise from hearsay but came from the official accounts of the US government. Hence, there was no concern about the veracity of the information. There should have been an instant public condemnation by the media of such an inept behaviour. However, no such news report was released. I do not believe that the media can use the argument of being too busy to check its information. Not commenting on these slurs almost amount to endorsement of such an intemperate language.

It seemed that the media was looking for an angle so that it could give an escape route to the former US president and his team for their foul language against a country and its PM.

[7]Ibid.

The Western media waited for Kissinger's conditional apology to publish the news item. A rather forced and conditional apology came from him on 2 July 2005. Only then did the media run headlines such as 'Kissinger Sorry for Deriding Mrs Gandhi' (*Guardian*),[8] 'Kissinger Regrets 1971 Remarks on India' (*New York Times*),[9] 'Kissinger Apologizes for '71 Remarks About I. Gandhi' (*Washington Post*),[10] 'Kissinger Regrets Deriding India's Leader' (*NBC News*),[11] and 'Kissinger Regrets India Comments' (*BBC News*).[12]

All these headlines have one thing in common—they focus on the apology tendered by Kissinger and not on the abuses hurled by the US officials. For the Western media, the act of abusing India was not newsworthy itself. Hence, for these publications, the big news was about Kissinger apologizing and not the foul and filthy language used by the then US president and his aides. These headlines raise serious questions about Western media's attitude towards India.

All the Western media publications mentioned above did not question the US government on this issue. All the reports were based on a secondary source instead of getting their correspondents to cover the story. A local Indian TV channel,

---

[8]Ramesh, Randeep, 'Kissinger Sorry for Deriding Mrs Gandhi', *Guardian,* 2 July, 2005, https://tinyurl.com/mrx83m2f. Accessed on 24 October 2023.

[9]'Kissinger Regrets 1971 Remarks on India', *New York Times,* 2 July, 2005, https://tinyurl.com/4jspkf87. Accessed on 24 October 2023.

[10]'Kissinger Apologizes for '71 Remarks about I. Gandhi', *Washington Post,* 2 July 2005, https://tinyurl.com/rz72yhtx. Accessed on 24 October 2023.

[11]'Kissinger Regrets Deriding India's Leader', *NBC News,* 1 July 2005, https://tinyurl.com/ym6mpurm. Accessed on 24 October 2023.

[12]'Kissinger Regrets India Comments', *BBC News,* 2 July 2005, https://tinyurl.com/musv6k9v. Accessed on 24 October 2023.

NDTV, sought Kissinger's reaction to such foul language.[13] International agencies picked the news from the channel and others just copied it. In the story, while apologizing for the foul language, Kissinger seemed to be rationalizing its use and said that it had to be seen 'in the context of the Cold War politics', with India being a Soviet ally.[14] However, all they seem to have done is reproduce identical reports quoting NDTV. This speaks volumes about their professionalism and ethical standards of these media outfits.

Imagine what would happen if such abuses were hurled against leaders of any of the Western countries by significant figures of a Third-World nation. I believe the Western media would create a hue and cry with reports, articles and editorials. It would describe this as uncivil, uncouth and uncultured behaviour and would demand an unconditional apology. There would be demands to stop all international aid to such a country, and any Third-World leader using such terms would have been named an international outcast and a persona non grata. But when the reverse happened, in this situation with President Nixon and Kissinger, no such thing happened. For them, the insult to a Third-World sovereign nation like India had no value; their bias towards their own government and leaders was quite evident here. The fact remains that the Western media did not react for three full

---

[13] India News, 'When Henry Kissinger Called Indira Gandhi a B***h, Indians "Bastards"', *NDTV,* 30 November 2023, https://tinyurl.com/53tzwbdx. Accessed on 1 December 2023.

[14] 'Kissinger Regrets Deriding India's Leader', *NBC News,* 1 July 2005, https://tinyurl.com/ym6mpurm. Accessed on 24 October 2023.

days after declassification of the documents. What should have been a top headline news item was completely ignored and overlooked.[15]

Banning of the BBC

The Western media, including the BBC, has often carried the official agenda of the Western powers. This was the trend even in the early 1970s, when Indira Gandhi's government had a spat with the UK broadcaster. Prime Minister Indira was so enraged with the BBC's reporting that she ordered the closure of its offices in India. In fact, PM Indira banned the BBC in India twice during her tenure.[16]

The first time the BBC was banned had to do with a mini documentary series directed by Louis Malle called Phantom India. Many, including the GoI, believed that the series painted a biased picture of India. He also directed a documentary called *Calcutta*, which was criticized by none other than the Oscar-winning filmmaker Satyajit Ray. He questioned Malle's motivations.[17] Malle's take on poverty, slums and rituals in the city sparked debates in India. The issue also came up for discussion in Indian Parliament. *Calcutta* was telecast on 10 June. The the GoI took up the

---

[15]'150. Conversation Among President Nixon, the President's Assistant for National Security Affairs (Kissinger), and the President's Assistant (Haldeman)', Foreign Relations of the United States, 1969–1976, Volume E–7, Documents on South Asia, 1969–1972, Office of the Historian, Foreign Service Institute, United States Department of State, https://tinyurl.com/yc26d2vj. Accessed on 11 December 2023.

[16]Mukhopadhyay, Sounak, 'When Indira Gandhi Banned BBC…Twice', *Mint*, 17 February 2023, https://tinyurl.com/ys24jx4d. Accessed on 24 October 2023.

[17]Ibid.

matter with Government of UK and the BBC. However, the broadcaster continued weekly screening of the series in July. The GoI made a statement on the floor of Lok Sabha on 27 August, describing these films as anti-India. The deputy minister for external affairs back then, Surendra Pal Singh, announced, 'The House is aware that in recent months there has been dissatisfaction and adverse comment in the country, in the press and in the Parliament about BBC TV having shown several films which portray India. Its life and culture in a tendentious and distorted manner.'[18] Prime Minister Indira's government banned the BBC a second time again during Emergency in 1975.[19]

BBC in the Soup

There have been many other occasions when the BBC's conduct came up for criticism in Indian Parliament. In June 1984, the BBC aired the notorious interview with the Khalistani leader Jagjit Singh Chauhan. In this interview, he openly called for the beheading of PM Indira and her family.[20] Parliamentarians across party lines were agitated because of this interview that incited violence against an elected and sitting PM of the country. When it came up for discussion in the Rajya Sabha, members alleged that the BBC was carrying out an anti-India propaganda. One member said:

[18]Lok Sabha Debates, Fourth Session, No. 22, *Parliament Archives,* 27 August 1970, p. 207, http://tinyurl.com/sj6usw96. Accessed on 15 December 2023.

[19]Divya A., 'The Journey of BBC in India, and Its Run-ins with Various Governments', *Indian Express,* 16 February 2023, https://tinyurl.com/2x5afstp. Accessed on 20 November 2023.

[20]Ramesh, Randeep, 'Jagjit Singh Chauhan', *Guardian,* 10 April 2007, https://tinyurl.com/mrxac9ew. Accessed on 24 October 2023.

> The BBC's anti-India role at the time of Indo-China war in 1962, Indo-Pak war in 1965, communal clashes or any internal disturbances in a vast country like that of ours is very well known. Sir, as a matter of fact, the BBC not only exploited such occurrences, but has been doing everything it can to create hatred among our people, encourage terrorists, incite violence and accentuate such troubles.[21]

A few months after the inflammatory BBC interview, PM Indira was assassinated by her Sikh bodyguards in October 1984.

A pertinent question to ask here is: should the BBC have aired such an interview, which openly called for the assassination of a leader, that too the PM of a democracy like India? Does it not breach common journalistic norms? Should they have not apologized for telecasting such a violent utterance? Would they have allowed such an interview against the PM of the UK?

There have been many other occasions when the BBC has painted India, Indian products and Indian customs in poor light.[22] Whenever the GoI has lodged its objection with the BBC, the UK government, very conveniently, has taken a stand that the BBC is an autonomous entity.[23] However, PM Indira never believed that the BBC was autonomous. She

---

[21]Nand Kishore Bhatt, MP, Oral Answers, Rajya Sabha Debates, *Parliament Archives,* 2 August 1984, p. 9.

[22]Lok Sabha Debates, Seventh Series, Volume XXX, No. 55, *Parliament Archives,* 7 May 1981, pp. 243, 289, 297, 301, http://tinyurl.com/ykmytv29. Accessed on 15 December 2023.

[23]Lok Sabha Debates, Fourth Session, No. 22, *Parliament Archives,* 27 August 1970, p. 207, http://tinyurl.com/sj6usw96. Accessed on 15 December 2023.

once declared in Parliament:

> I do not want to enter into a discussion about how autonomous the BBC is. We know that on some occasions, it has gone against its own Government. But on other occasions, it also does, specially, in foreign policy matters, sometimes conform to its government's directives. This is not the case with only the BBC; this is so with most of the Press and the media abroad.[24]

WESTERN MEDIA AND ATAL BIHARI VAJPAYEE

US Hypocrisy on Terrorism in India

India has been facing terrorism since the 1980s. Its presence started in Punjab and later spread to Jammu and Kashmir. It originates from and is abated by Pakistan. The West and its media have always looked at this issue from the West's parochial interests rather than treating terrorism as a global menace. Several instances can be cited of moments when India faced terror attacks and the West looked the other way because directly condemnation of the perpetrators of such attacks did not suit the West. One such instance also stands as a shining example of double speak of the West and its media. It was during the reign of Atal Bihari Vajpayee as the PM.

Armed Pakistani terrorists attacked Indian Parliament on 13 December 2001. The winter session of Parliament was on and the top leadership, including the PM, was inside

---

[24]Indira Gandhi, Oral Answers, Rajya Sabha Debates, *Parliament Archives,* 2 August 1984, p. 10.

Parliament building. The terrorists had planned to take the Indian leadership hostage. Thankfully, all five attackers who had entered the premises were killed within half an hour by the security forces. However, the country was rightly enraged. Parliament building is considered a symbol of Indian democracy. Attacking it symbolized attacking the very edifice of democratic values and system. Prime Minister Vajpayee was enraged at this attempt and announced Operation Parakram.[25] The Indian Army was asked to move to the border. Pakistan also was forced to move its forces to the border, and both the armies almost clashed with each other.[26]

Prime Minister Vajpayee declared that 'the punishment will be as big as the crime'.[27] At that time, the US government advised India to share intelligence inputs with Pakistani agencies while praising the then president of Pakistan, Parvez Musharraf, for his commitment to eradicate terrorism. The then US Secretary of State Colin Powell stated, 'We hope that India will share all the information that they have acquired concerning this—this tragedy in their parliament building in New Delhi with the Pakistanis.'[28]

The USA exposed its double standards with this statement. It had ruled out any talks or negotiations with those responsible for the 9/11 attacks in New York, but

---

[25]Coll, Steve, 'The Stand-Off', *New Yorker,* 5 February, 2006, https://tinyurl.com/rypbd5px. Accessed on 20 November 2023.

[26]TNN, 'Parliament Attack Had brought India, Pak on Brink of Another War', *Times of India,* 10 February 2013, http://tinyurl.com/3d5jawav. Accessed on 20 November 2023.

[27]'India-Pakistan Tension Rise Following Parliament Attack', *PBS Newshour,* 18 December 2001, https://tinyurl.com/2f5yyr2c. Accessed on 24 October 2023.

[28]Ibid.

here it was advising Indian leadership to share all details with Pakistani agencies that were suspected to be behind that terror attack. This double standard was not limited only to the US policymakers. Its media also followed the same hypocrisy. It would describe Al Qaeda leaders as terrorists but would call those responsible for attacks against India as Islamic extremists. The term 'Islamic extremist' is more nuanced and politically acceptable than 'terrorist' and carries less severe connotations. So, when Western media houses used this and other such terms for terrorists targeting India and other countries, they downplayed the severity of the situation.

A cursory look at the headlines of major Western media publications after the attack on Indian Parliament illustrates their biases well. The *Washington Post* called them 'gunmen,'[29] the BBC called them 'militants,'[30] the *Guardian* described them as 'Kashmiri separatists,'[31] the *New York Times* described the Lashkar-e-Tayyaba as a Pakistan-based separatist group,[32] and *PBS News* described Pakistan-based Lashkar-e-Tayyaba and Jaish-e-Mohammed as 'separatist guerilla groups.'[33] None

---

[29]Lakshmi, Rama, 'Gunmen with Explosives Attack Indian Parliament,' *Washington Post,* 14 December 2001, https://tinyurl.com/3n9w94vf. Accessed on 24 October 2023.

[30]'Indian Parliament Attack Kills 12,' *BBC News,* 13 December 2001, https://tinyurl.com/y7tkwzfb. Accessed on 24 October 2023.

[31]Miglani, Sanjeev, '12 Die in Indian Parliament Attack,' *Guardian,* 14 December 2001, https://tinyurl.com/yz27jrxz. Accessed on 24 October 2023.

[32]Reuters, 'India Blames Pakistani Groups for Parliament Attack,' *New York Times,* 14 December 2001, https://tinyurl.com/34k2bs24. Accessed on 24 October 2023.

[33]'India-Pakistan Tension Rise Following Parliament Attack,' *PBS Newshour,* 18 December 2001, https://tinyurl.com/2f5yyr2c. Accessed on 24 October 2023.

of these publications referred to the attackers as terrorists.

To a lay reader, usually the terms 'terrorist', 'extremist' and 'gunmen' might mean more or less the same. However, how a media house uses these terms shows its political leaning. Many Western publications describe terror attacks in India and other countries as per their political orientation. The BBC, for example, uses different yardsticks on such occasions. Recently, the BBC's world affairs editor John Simpson, while addressing the issue of why the media house refuses to call Hamas gunmen 'terrorists' said, 'The answer goes right back to the BBC's founding principles. Terrorism is a loaded word, which people use about an outfit they disapprove of morally. It's simply not the BBC's job to tell people who to support and who to condemn—who are the good guys and who are the bad guys.'[34] This is the same logic that justifies calling Kashmiri and Khalistani separatists 'extremists' instead of 'terrorists.'[35]

However, this moral high ground that the BBC takes is highly subjective. The BBC has called members of the Irish Republican Army (IRA) 'terrorists.'[36] More recently, it has called the 9/11 attacks as terror attacks.[37] The reason behind the BBC identifying only attacks on the West as terrorist

---

[34]Simpson, John, 'Why BBC Doesn't Call Hamas Militants "Terrorists" - John Simpson', *BBC News,* 11 October 2023, http://tinyurl.com/mr3n8eu5. Accessed on 15 December 2023.

[35]'Pulwama Attack: India Mourns Kashmir Dead', *BBC News,* 16 February 2019, http://tinyurl.com/yskfhjdm. Accessed on 15 December 2023.

[36]O'Neill, Julian and Niall Glynn, 'Northern Ireland Terrorism Threat Level Rises', *BBC News,* 28 March 2023, http://tinyurl.com/yc7ccw55. Accessed on 15 December 2023.

[37]'9/11 Anniversary: How the World Reacted to Terror Attacks', *BBC News,* 10 September 2021, http://tinyurl.com/3rcp6djk. Accessed on 15 December 2023.

activity but not ones on the rest of the world (for example, the attack on Pulwama) remains obscure.[38]

Shifting the Narrative

During this time, the USA was fixated on Afghanistan in the aftermath of 9/11 attacks. It wanted to hunt down Osama Bin Laden and Al Qaeda, and Pakistan agreed to facilitate and host American forces on its soil. Moving the Pakistan Army from the Afghanistan–Pakistan border to the Indo-Pak border did not suit US interests.[39] So, it sided with Pakistan instead of India. In an attempt to divert people's attention from the assault on India's temple of democracy, the Western media started publishing stories alluding to an impending nuclear war between India and Pakistan.

An article published in the *Washington Post* on 29 December 2001 is full of advice to India for caution and restraint.[40] India's anger at that time was described as 'saber rattling' to indicate that the Indian leadership was itching for war. There were stories that said that 12 million people could die in case of a nuclear war between two South Asian neighbours.[41] These stories were fed by the US intelligence

---

[38]'Kashmir Attack: Bomb Kills 40 Indian Paramilitary Police in Convoy', *BBC News,* 14 February 2019, http://tinyurl.com/yc7d7t8d. Accessed on 15 December 2023.

[39]Coll, Steve, 'The Stand-Off', *New Yorker,* 5 February 2006, https://tinyurl.com/rypbd5px. Accessed on 20 November 2023.

[40]Allen, Mike and Peter Slevin, 'Bush Presses India, Pakistan to Ease Conflict', *Washington Post,* 29 December 2001, http://tinyurl.com/26zacpkw. Accessed on 3 January 2024.

[41]Shanker, Tom, '12 Million Could Die at Once in an India-Pakistan Nuclear War', *New York Times,* 27 May 2002, http://tinyurl.com/2s4vsahv. Accessed on 26 October 2023.

sources. Similar stories appeared in the *New York Times*, the *Guardian* and other publications in May 2002.[42] Surprisingly, none of these stories mentioned the terror attack on Indian Parliament. The narrative was shifted from terrorism to the likely war. In this scenario, India was painted as the likely aggressor. India, which was a victim of terrorism, was almost described as a war monger.

While there always is a danger of escalation when it comes to any conflict, Indian officials were very clear that this was not the case. India and Pakistan are nuclear-armed countries, but that did not have to mean that India would choose the nuclear warfare route to retaliate Pakistani terrorism. It has made clear that it will never be the first one to use nuclear weapons. After the 1998 nuclear test, India enunciated a doctrine of 'No First Use' (NFU) of nuclear weapons. Instead, the threat of nuclear attack was a blackmail tactic used by Pakistani leadership. India's national security advisor, Brajesh Mishra, called it a Pakistani bluff. He said India was too big, and in case Pakistan used tactical nuclear weapons, its entire survival would be at risk.[43]

Pakistan weaponized nuclear deterrence and kept on using terrorism as an instrument of state policy. The Western media happily obliged it by publishing horrific scenarios of what it thought could be a likely nuclear war

---

[42]Harding, Luke and Rory McCarthy, 'Why Nuclear Conflict Is a Real Threat', *Guardian*, 23 May 2002, http://tinyurl.com/53rzuxfy. Accessed on 15 December 2023; Sipress, Alan and Thomas E. Ricks, 'Report: India, Pakistan Were Near Nuclear War in '99', *Washington Post*, http://tinyurl.com/37cmzema. Accessed on 15 December 2023; Shanker, Tom, '12 Million Could Die at Once in an India-Pakistan Nuclear War', *New York Times*, 27 May 2002, http://tinyurl.com/2s4vsahv. Accessed on 26 October 2023.
[43]Ibid.

between India and Pakistan. Unsurprisingly, none of these stories mentioned the terror attack on Indian Parliament. The narrative was totally shifted from terrorism to the likely war. In this scenario, India was painted as a likely aggressor. India who was a victim of terrorism was almost described as a war monger.

The US media knew and conveyed the scenario of a nuclear war that had been playing on the mind of the West. As a result, the US leadership created diplomatic and other pressures on India, which could not withstand it.[44] Finally, India withdrew its forces from the border in October 2002. This fulfilled the Western strategic objectives without disturbing its close ally, Pakistan.

This was not the first time that the argument of a possible nuclear conflict was used by the Western media. It was also used during the Kargil War in 1999.[45] This, in fact, is an oft-repeated story that the Western media kept on resurrecting till as recently as 2019, during the Pulwama terror attack. *The Atlantic* published a story in March 2019 titled 'The Other Nuclear Threat.'[46] However, the Modi government called this bluff with surgical strikes; it did so in September 2016 and at the time of the Balakot air raids in February 2019.

One has to see that the Western press cherry picks

---

[44]'India to Pull Troops from Pakistan Border', *CNN,* 16 October 2002, http://tinyurl.com/3txk52zw. Accessed on 15 December 2023.

[45]Sipress, Alan and Thomas E. Ricks, 'Report: India, Pakistan Were Near Nuclear War in '99', *Washington Post,* http://tinyurl.com/37cmzema. Accessed on 15 December 2023.

[46]White, Joshua T., 'The Other Nuclear Threat', *Atlantic,* 5 March 2019, http://tinyurl.com/msz94y2z. Accessed on 3 January 2024.

an argument that suits the larger strategic interests of its governments; it doesn't matter who is at the helm of affairs in India at that particular time. The instances cited above are from different times with two different governments in India. Indira Gandhi was a Congress leader and Atal Bihari Vajpayee was a Bharatiya Janata Party (BJP) leader. The BJP has been described by many in the Western media as a Hindu nationalist party.[47] However, even though the PMs came from different political backgrounds, the Western English media used the same template. When it comes to India, be it Gandhi, Sardar Patel, Indira, Vajpayee or Modi, the Western media uses the same lens to look at them. It has a narrative that works as per the West's own interest and objectives. The Western media simply acts as a tool to further larger policy goals of the Western bloc.

India and other countries have been victims of such selective reporting by the so-called independent media outfits that are touted as temples of authenticity and credibility. These half-truths become very dangerous when the countries are in crisis situations.

Reporting during crises becomes very crucial for moulding the general opinion. First, the consumption of news content increases as the hunger for information grows during such times. Second, people tend to cling to only pieces of information, creating doubts. It's common

[47] This oversimplification also comes from the Western media's lack of proper understanding of the Indian political landscape as it only thinks in binaries. However, that is a separate issue altogether and needs deeper research and study.

for people to believe rumours and gossip that heighten the sense of insecurity during this time. Media creates a crisis of confidence in the system and leadership. Also, people tend to believe in 'foreign sources' during these times. Media in general and so-called independent and foreign media in particular thrive during crises. They appropriate the vantage point and create a narrative suited to them. It shapes the narratives and impacts the responses and behaviour of people during crises.

The Western media outfits have built a narrative for themselves by creating a false halo of impartiality, credibility and factual reporting. They are very opinionated and subjective in their approach. Their reports come in handy for the powerful international interests and lobbies that try to put politically unfavourable local regimes in a corner to achieve their commercial, strategic and geopolitical objectives. The media becomes an active tool in such situations. We may recall how the Western media was embedded in the campaign of creating a false weapons of mass destruction (WMD) narrative in Iraq in 2003. Not only did the media carry the narrative, a few of them like the *Economist* went to the extent of calling for a war. It clearly announced that 'our vote is for war.'[48] The Western embedded media was as much responsible for creating this illusive and imaginary threat from WMD as the US administration led by the then president George Bush.

---

[48]Reuters, 'The Case for War,' *Economist,* 1 August 2002, http://tinyurl.com/yeuuc4f2. Accessed on 15 December 2023.

Chapter 4

THE ELITE SPACE CLUB

The disdain for India in Western societies and the manufactured narratives about it run much deeper than the spoken or the written word. They have impacted India's history, they are affecting its present and they will have a large bearing on the future. For substantiation, one can pick up any British or American newspaper and read the articles on India.

Often, one has to read in between the lines to understand the intent. It is hard to pinpoint at times, but the sense of superiority of the writer is conveyed in a very subtle manner. One notices that even when there is a positive story about India and its achievement, the writer tends to sprinkle it with a negative data point or unnecessary sarcasm, many a times unrelated with the story. An example is a Reuters story filed after Indian athletes won record medals in Hangzhou Asian Games in China in October 2023. India won 107 medals and placed fourth in the tally. It was the country's best performance so far. India had finished eighth with 70 medals in the earlier edition of the Asian Games in Jakarta, Indonesia, five years prior. This was a great leap forward for Indian athletes. There was an all-round applause for them all over the country. However, the international news agency Reuters filed a story titled 'India Upbeat after Becoming a Bigger Fish in Small Asian Pool'.[1] The title of the story not only belittled India's sporting efforts but also ridiculed it. Anyone remotely connected with sports would have lauded sportspersons efforts for a great jump in the medal tally, but Reuters decided to make fun of it.

Why does it happen? Why does the Western media do it time and again? Its roots lie in our engagement with the West, especially the British, who credit themselves with 'creating the modern world as it stands today'.[2]

Britain was the greatest power during the last century. In a way, it represented the Western world as far as India was concerned. After World War II, many of the colonies, including India, were able to free themselves from the clutches of imperial control. Since then, Britain has consistently made efforts to find some other way to maintain its sway over these countries. Today, the UK, USA and European Union (EU) are making this effort together as a force, and the media has become one of the sharpest weapons in their arsenal to control their former colonies.

The popular Western imagination continues to suffer from its inability to accept the Third-World nations giving them competition in fields where they once reigned supreme.

---

[1]Ransom, Ian, 'India Upbeat after Becoming Bigger Fish in Small Asian Pool', *Reuters Sports,* 5 October 2023, http://tinyurl.com/3awwedx9. Accessed on 15 December 2023.

[2]Ferguson, Niall, *Empire: How Britain Made the Modern World,* Penguin Books, 2004.

The *New York Times*'s reaction to the success of Mangalyaan is a case in hand.

THE NEW YORK TIMES RIDICULED MANGALYAAN

The misconception is so deep in the Western psyche that when India's Mangalyaan reached Mars orbit in September 2014, one of the most popular US newspapers published a nasty cartoon mocking the achievement.[3] It was an illustration of a poor farmer, knocking on the door of the 'Elite Space Club' with a cow. Meanwhile, the two people in the club are drinking wine and reading a newspaper story about India's Mars mission, too shocked and hesitant to open the door. What was a great moment of pride for India, as it became the fourth nation in the world to achieve this feat, was ridiculed by the newspaper. The Western media also mocked the mission's budget, which the *New York Times* described as a shoestring.[4]

In response to these Western narratives, the journalist Sharnaya Haridas wrote an article in *Huffpost* calling the cartoon racist.[5] She pointed out that all the members depicted in the elite space club are male, white and wealthy. Maybe the editor found the farmer-and-cow stereotype portrayed

---

[3]Haridas, Sharanya, 'The "New York Times" Publishes Racist Comic About India's Space Mission', *Huffpost,* 30 September 2014, https://tinyurl.com/2apcfyze. Accessed on 20 November 2023.

[4]Harris, G., 'On a Shoestring, India Sends Its Orbiter to Mars on Its First Try', *New York Times,* 24 September 2014, http://tinyurl.com/yckfpppb. Accessed on 15 December 2023.

[5]Haridas, Sharanya, 'The "'New York Times"' Publishes Racist Comic About India's Space Mission', *Huffpost,* 30 September 2014, https://tinyurl.com/2apcfyze. Accessed on 20 November 2023.

by the cartoon funny. However, there was nothing humorous about it. The cartoon, indeed, was in poor taste and lacked sensitivity.

The *New York Times* later apologized for the cartoon. 'We apologise to readers who were offended by the choice of images in this cartoon,' wrote Andrew Rosenthal, editorial page editor of the *New York Times*, in a Facebook post. He explained, 'The intent of the cartoonist, Heng Kim Song, was to highlight how space exploration is no longer the exclusive domain of rich, Western countries.'[6]

The apology of the *New York Times* notwithstanding, the imagery used made the perception of the West towards India clear. The country's depiction as a poor, rural man trying to enter the exclusive elite club of the Western world is not a mere coincidence. That the Western elite is in suits and the Indian farmer is in his dhoti depicts a mindset that perceives the developing countries in a fundamentally skewed manner. The members of the 'Elite Space Club' remind us of colonial masters who are all very 'civilized.' The undertone of the cartoon seems to say, '*How dare a dhoti-clad half-naked fakir*[7] *enter into this exclusive and predominantly white domain?*'

The *New York Times* is not alone in this tirade of negativity

---

[6]'India Mars Mission: New York Times Apologises for Cartoon,' *BBC News*, 6 October 2014, http://tinyurl.com/422vdfsa. Accessed on 15 December 2023.

[7]Winston Churchill had described the Indian leader Gandhi as a 'half-naked fakir.' He had said: 'It is [...] alarming and also nauseating to see Mr. Gandhi, a seditious middle temple lawyer, now posing as a fakir of a type well known in the East, striding half-naked up the steps of the Vice-regal palace, while he is still organizing and conducting a defiant campaign of civil disobedience, to parlay on equal terms with the representative of the King-Emperor.' See James, R.R. (ed.), *Winston S. Churchill: His Complete Speeches, 1897–1963*, Volume 5, Chelsea House, New York, 1974, p. 4985.

towards India. After the success of the Mars mission, Mangalyaan, in September 2014, the BBC did a story titled 'Mangalyaan: India's Race for Space Success'.[8] The story was essentially on the scientific success of India's space agency, the Indian Space Research Organisation (ISRO). However, after enumerating the successes, the writer inserted a subheading calling the Mangalyaan success 'delusional dreams'. While the reporter could not find a point of valid criticism in eight paragraphs under the subheading, they wrote a three-line paragraph claiming 'many say' that it is a 'delusional dream'. And then, they almost compulsorily added that 400 million Indians live without electricity and 600 million do not have access to toilets. The writer doesn't cite any sources for these numbers. They do not explain what was delusional about India's space ambitions. They do not throw any light on why they thought so. This raises many questions: who are the 'many' saying such things? Why did the writer hide behind such anonymous sources? Since no one is quoted here, it is safe to assume that these are actually the biased minds of the BBC establishment that probably forced the writer to add unrelated negative lines in an otherwise positive story.

The fact is, India may have reached Mars, Indians might be reaching top positions in the world's leading companies,[9] India may have inoculated a record number of its citizens with internally produced Covid-19 vaccines in a very

---

[8]'Mangalyaan: India's Race to Space Success', *BBC News,* 24 September 2014, http://tinyurl.com/y5j97sy8. Accessed on 15 December 2023.

[9]Kalita, S.M., '9 Reasons the Indian CEO Keeps Coming to the Rescue', *CNN Business,* 4 February 2020, http://tinyurl.com/4rxmk335. Accessed on 15 December 2023.

short time,[10] the launch of Chandrayaan-3 may have cost lesser than many Hollywood movies,[11] but the dominant Western narrative will still doubt its credentials. From da Gama in 1542 to Churchill in the 1930s to the *New York Times* in 2014 and beyond, the Western imagery of India has consisted persistently of the half-naked village folk and remains concentrated only on denigrations, denunciations, conflicts and crises. The launch of Chandrayaan series of moon missions is another case in point.

CHANDRAYAAN COVERAGE BY THE BRITISH MEDIA

Be it the Chandrayaan; launch of satellites for itself and for other nations; or Mangalyaan, the Mars mission, ISRO has made its mark on space exploration with a high degree of success and at very affordable costs. In fact, its low-cost-high-output model has made it a formidable competitor in space launches.[12] Indian Space Research Organisation's launch of Chandrayaan-3 has been lauded by the world.[13] It is significant because it explored the south

---

[10]Roy, R., 'India Hits One Billion Covid-19 Vaccines Administered', *The Wall Street Journal,* 21 October 2021, http://tinyurl.com/2r4jczs6. Accessed on 15 December 2023.

[11]'India's Mars Mission was Cheaper than All These Hollywood Movies', *NBC News,* 6 October 2014, http://tinyurl.com/ytkfw72m. Accessed on 15 December 2023.

[12]'The Secret behind India's Budget-Friendly Moonshots: How ISRO Has Developed Its Low-Cost Edge', *Economic Times,* 24 August 2023, https://tinyurl.com/mr3xkzkz. Accessed on 20 November 2023.

[13]Ghosh, Poulomi, 'Rover Pragyan Takes a Walk on Moon: "Made in India Made for Moon"', *Hindustan Times,* 24 August 2023, http://tinyurl.com/mprn75ay. Accessed on 15 December 2023.

pole of the moon, a site that had not been explored until then. It becomes more significant because the Russians had failed at a similar mission just before the soft landing of the Chandrayaan-3. For many reasons, the successful launch of Chandrayaan-3 and preceding missions were a matter of jubilation and pride for India, but not so for some in the Western media, especially the BBC, where one news anchor made some condescending remarks about India.

BBC Anchor: Mother of Loaded Questions

The resounding success of Chandrayaan-3 had been preceded by two other launches, one of which was of Chandrayaan-2. While the first lander and rover linked with the Chandrayaan-2 mission crashed on the surface of the moon, they had still provided vital learnings, which aided the success of Chandrayaan-3.[14] As India was preparing for the launch of Chandrayaan-2, BBC anchor Aaron Heslehurst could not find it in him to describe what Chandrayaan was doing for India and the world. In fact, he ended up discovering a dark and racist side of himself with a heavily loaded question to BBC correspondent Nitin Srivastava. This was his exact question:

> You know, I have to ask because many people would be thinking about this. India, a country that lacks a lot of infrastructure, a country that has extreme poverty, I think more than 700 million Indians do not have access to a toilet, really, should they really be spending this kind of money on a space programme?[15]

---

[14]'India Lands on Moon: How Is Chandrayaan-3 Different from Chandrayaan-2?', *Hindustan Times,* 23 August 2023, https://tinyurl.com/yckbpx3u. Accessed on 20 November 2023.

[15]@MeghUpdates, *X* (formerly Twitter), 23 August 2023, 6.53 p.m.,

This question betrays a complete lack of understanding about what ISRO has done for the common Indian. It is an ill-researched and deliberate running down of India as a nation.

The BBC anchor's comment was bizarre, to say the least. He seemed to suggest that no investment should be made in science, education and development till every person is not uplifted from poverty and till the basic facilities are available to each and every citizen in a country. His superficial argument bears no understanding of how humanity has developed through the ages. The fact is that development of societies seldom takes place in a linear fashion. Heslehurst's condescending remark on India and its poverty is also absurd considering the state of Britain's own economy. Not many people know about this because the Western media refuses to put it up on the board that 20 per cent of Britain in 2021 was living in poverty. That totals up to 1.34 crore British citizens![16]

Other Misleading Reports by British Media

Another British TV anchor, Patrick Christys, went on a similar tirade on GBNews. He said that he would like to congratulate India on landing on the dark side of the moon and would also like to invite India to return the '2.3 billion GBP Foreign aid that Britain government gave between 2016 to 2021.'[17] Christy then proceeded to urge that the British

---

https://tinyurl.com/yekhd68z. Accessed on 20 November 2023.

[16]'UK Poverty 2023: The Essential Guide to Understand Poverty in the UK', *Joseph Rowntree Foundation,* 26 January 2023, http://tinyurl.com/4ytbnbdb. Accessed on 15 December 2023.

[17]GBNews, '"India, Give Us Back Our £2 BILLION" | Patrick Christys Says

taxpayer should keep hold of this 'British aid' and suggested that Britain should not give any money to countries with a space programme as a rule, adding that if any nation can afford to fire a rocket at the dark side of the moon, it 'should not be coming to us for a handout'.[18] He then painted the picture of India as the fifth largest economy with an annual GDP of $3.75 trillion, and rhetorically asked why Britain was helping poverty-stricken Indians when their own government was not bothered.

However, this 'aid' is more beneficial to the aid-giver than the recipient country. It always has strings attached, which serve deep foreign policy and strategic objectives of the developed world. An article in the *Guardian* reveals that any aid given to India must measure up to the principles of democracy and human rights as defined by the aid giver.[19] These principles are mostly politically motivated and tied to geopolitics. The perception created by the media ultimately becomes fodder for internal British politics, where some leaders use it to create vote banks.

We see former UK Independence Party Leader Nigel Farage doing this. He demanded that Britain should not be giving 'a penny' to India after the Chandrayaan-3 launch.[20] Many local British newspapers picked the story from the

---

Rocket Means They Don't Need UK Money', *YouTube,* 23 August 2023, https://tinyurl.com/akynh9bv. Accessed on 20 November 2023.

[18]Ibid.

[19]'UK Aid to India Does Little for Human Rights and Democracy, Watchdog Finds', *Guardian,* 14 March 2023, http://tinyurl.com/yc2vmc7e. Accessed on 17 October 2023.

[20]'Nigel Farage Says UK Should Not Be Giving "A Penny" to India after Moon Landing', *Express,* 24 August 2023, http://tinyurl.com/2t7u28xr. Accessed on 18 October 2023.

broadcast. Farage further stated that while half of India lives below the poverty line, the country is spending money on space programmes, nuclear weapons and the military. This is a reiteration of the Western media propaganda that scientific progress and poverty alleviation cannot go hand in hand.

However, a statement by a spokesperson of the British foreign office demolishes the facade of 'aid' that Christys relies on for his argument. The *Guardian* reports the spokesperson saying, 'Since 2015 the UK has given no financial aid to the the GoI. Most of our funding now is focused on business investments which help create new markets and jobs for the UK, as well as India. UK investments are also helping tackle shared challenges such as climate change.'[21]

BRITAIN IS RESPONSIBLE FOR POVERTY IN INDIA

A statement by the industrialist Anand Mahindra summarized India's reaction to Heslehurst's video very aptly. He said that the BBC and the British will never understand the feelings of pride that such achievements bring for India. In a tweet, he said that apart from wealth, the most important thing that the British looted during the colonial subjugation was the sense of pride and respect. Such scientific achievements bring back that self-belief. He also rightly added that the BBC anchor should have known that it was the British who were responsible for poverty in India, which is now a well-documented fact.[22]

---

[21]'UK Aid to India Does Little for Human Rights and Democracy, Watchdog Finds', *Guardian,* 14 March 2023, http://tinyurl.com/yc2vmc7e. Accessed on 17 October 2023.

[22]'Chandrayaan-3: Anand Mahindra Slams British Anchor for Remarks about

Evidence of British Exploitation

The Angus Maddison Research report, published in 2001, records India's contribution to the global GDP before and during imperialism. As per this research, India's share in the world GDP was 22.6 per cent in 1600 and 24.4 per cent in 1700. It started decreasing after the British started their indiscriminate exploitation of Indian resources. The planned destruction of Indian industry, agriculture and the self-sufficient village economy led to the flight of Indian wealth, and India's share in world GDP was reduced to 16 per cent in 1820 during the Company Raj. It reached 12.2 per cent in 1870 after the British government took direct control of the country after the First War of Independence. India's share in world GDP further reduced to a paltry 4.2 per cent in 1950 when the British ultimately left India.[23] It is clear that during their time in India, the British treated the Indian economy like a goldmine to be looted and exited after plundering it.

However, Maddison was not the first one to document the Indian economy's targeted destruction by the British. Much earlier, American author and journalist Will Durant had written a book titled *The Case for India* in 1930, in which he identified the British exploitation of India. He states, 'Britain's conscious and deliberate bleeding of India [was the] greatest crime in all history.'[24] Durant visited India

---

India's Poverty, Toilets, Says "It Helps Restore…"', *Mint,* 24 August 2023, http://tinyurl.com/yc5jn7uh. Accessed on 15 December 2023.

[23]Maddison, A., *The World Economy: A Millennial Perspective,* Development Centre Studies, OECD Publishing, Paris, 2001, p. 263.

[24]Durant, Will, *The Case for India,* Simon and Schuster, New York, 1930.

and witnessed the cruel oppression and the great suffering of people. He rebutted the British narrative that India was poor because it was overpopulated and Hindus were superstitious by stating, 'This exhaustion and starvation (of Indians) are due not, as their beneficiaries claim, to overpopulation and superstition, but to the most sordid and criminal exploitation of one nation by another in all recorded history.'[25]

This was also the time when the issue of giving self-rule to Indians was being debated in England and the Round Table Conference was being planned. Those opposing the self-rule had argued that Indians were not capable of managing their own affairs. Durant lambasted this imperial and racist argument and advocated self-rule by saying, 'England has year by year been bleeding India to the point of death, and that self-the GoI by the Hindus could not, within any reasonable probability, have worse results than the present form of alien domination.'[26]

POVERTY REDUCTION AND SCIENTIFIC PROGRESS GO HAND IN HAND

Many in the West care about poverty in India. Many tourists from abroad are hit by the stark difference between the developed and developing, poor and elite areas of cities as well as the abject poverty in some areas. However, when India has been taking giant strides in space technology, nuclear, defence, AI, the Internet of Things (IoT) and blockchain technology, it does not mean that it has been

[25]Ibid. 1–2.
[26]Ibid.

turning a blind eye towards the poor. In fact, from the Green Revolution to the satellite-launching endeavours, all are primarily aimed at providing food security to millions of Indians. There is no contradiction between poverty reduction programmes and investment in science, connectivity, infrastructure, technology and industry. These are complementary—one feeds the other.

India has 'Halved Its Poverty in 15 Years'

The global Multidimensional Poverty Index (MPI), released by the UN Development Programme (UNDP) in 2023, and the Oxford Poverty and Human Development Initiative (OPHI) at the University of Oxford highlight how India has been reducing poverty at a rapid pace. The report said that India has successfully halved its global MPI values within 15 years. It further adds, 'Notably, India saw a remarkable reduction in poverty, with 415 million people exiting poverty within a span of just 15 years (2005/6–19/21).'[27] According to the report, people who are multidimensionally poor and deprived under the nutrition indicator in India fell from a high of 44.3 per cent in 2005–06 to 11.8 per cent in 2019–21. Child mortality rates are also showing a remarkable improvement as they have fallen from 4.5 per cent to 1.5 per cent. This is a work in progress. It is believed that if India continues to grow at the rate of 7 per cent for 25 years, then it could eradicate poverty by 2050.[28]

---

[27]'415 Million Indians Came Out of Multidimensional Poverty in 15 Years, Says UNDP Study', *Hindu*, 26 July 2023, http://tinyurl.com/rh6xuv6j. Accessed on 15 December 2023.

[28]C. Rangarajan and D.K. Srivastava, 'A Roadmap to Eliminate Poverty in India', *Indian Express*, 19 July 2023, http://tinyurl.com/jypy2tkx. Accessed on

In a 2022 International Monetary Fund (IMF) study, it has been said that taking food subsidies into account, India has almost eliminated extreme poverty by 2020–21.[29] A separate World Bank working paper released in 2022 lauded India on the poverty front. The World Bank paper mentioned, 'India has more than halved the proportion of its extremely poor people—those earning below $1.9 by purchasing power parity a day—between 2011 and 2019. This would suggest the country is in sight of eradicating an historic scourge.'[30]

ISRO and the Hand that Feeds the World

Indian Space Research Organisation has done yeoman service to the common man of India. In fact, its contribution so far should be celebrated by the international community with awards and recognition. The space agency has helped increase India's agricultural produce and food security by creating technologies to enable agricultural land mapping, mapping of soil for availability of water, weather monitoring and fish mapping. India has the highest plant density in the world. According to The GoI's fourth advance estimate, India's food grain production in 2021–22 was 315.72 million tonnes.[31] India attained self-sufficiency in food production.[32]

---

15 December 2023.

[29]'India, No Longer a Poverty Posterboy', *Economic Times,* 18 April 2022, http://tinyurl.com/4m5y79sh. Accessed on 15 December 2023.

[30]Ibid.

[31]'Fourth Advance Estimate of Production of Foodgrains for 2021–22', *Press Information Bureau,* http://tinyurl.com/mvmjhhzm. Accessed on 15 December 2023.

[32]'India, Apart from being Self-Sufficient in Food Production, Has the Capacity to Meet the Food Requirements of a Large Part of the World: Shri Narendra Singh Tomar', *Press Information Bureau,* 20 September 2022,

India's food grain stocks proved very useful when the supply chain was disrupted in the wake of the Russia–Ukraine war. In a way, the same Indian farmers fed the world.[33] Hence, the Indian farmers may be considered a global asset, and ISRO's scientific development has helped farmers to increase their production.

Ease of Living for the Common Man

Scientific progress has made life easier for masses in India. The BBC anchor was ignorant of the fact that ease of living would not have been possible without the highly affordable space programmes and launch of communication satellites by ISRO. Affordable Internet access has revolutionized the Indian economy and society. This happened after Jio launched its 4G services in September 2016. In less than a decade, India has moved in a major way towards digital payments, tele-education, tele-medicine, financial inclusion and use of AI and blockchains in businesses. Not only has it made Indian businesses more efficient and internationally competitive, it has also helped increase ease of living for the common man. The Internet facility in India is one of the most cost-effective in the world.[34] In fact, in Pakistan, India's immediate neighbour, people pay twice the amount for the same amount of data, while in the US people pay 33 times

---

http://tinyurl.com/5bfy7tp9. Accessed on 16 September 2023.

[33]PTI, 'India's Wheat Exports Pick Up amid Russia-Ukraine War, Says Food Secy', *Business Standard,* 5 March 2022, http://tinyurl.com/5n776k6m. Accessed on 15 December 2023.

[34]'Mobile Data Price in India amongst Cheapest, Where It Is Less Costly than India?', *Mint,* 28 July 2022, http://tinyurl.com/27nf5zje. Accessed on 15 December 2023.

the money for the same.[35] Affordable Internet rates have not only ushered in a record number of Unicorns but have also opened up immense opportunities for those who are at the bottom of the pyramid.[36]

WHY IS THE WESTERN MEDIA TARGETING ISRO?

This is a question with complicated and multifaceted answers. Among many reasons, one is that of markets and competition. Dr Jitendra Singh, India's science and technology minister, stated, 'The cost of Chandrayaan-3 is merely Rs 600 crore, whereas a Hollywood film on space and moon costs more than Rs 600 crore.'[37]

Though this may appear as a jest, what he said is a fact. The cost of the Kevin Costner-starrer *John Carter*, after the adjustment of tax and interest, comes to around $264 million or ₹2,200 crore, which makes it about 3.6 times more expensive than Chandrayaan-3. Similarly, the cost of making the most expensive movie ever, *Avatar* (2009), was $324 million (₹2,700 crore), which is 4.5 times more than the cost of launching Chandrayaan-3.

Indian Space Research Organisation has launched 432 foreign satellites, out of which 397 were launched in the last 10 years. It earned $441 million as revenue from these

---

[35]Fleck, Anna, 'The Cost of Mobile Internet Around the World ', *Statista,* 9 January 2023, http://tinyurl.com/bdfk8wcb. Accessed on 15 December 2023.

[36]'Jio Completes Five Years of Operations; Tech World Congratulates', *Economic Times,* 6 September 2021, http://tinyurl.com/mrxrux3n. Accessed on 15 December 2023.

[37]'At Rs 600 Cr Chandrayaan-3 Costs Less than Some Hollywood films: Minister', *Business Standard,* 25 August 2023, http://tinyurl.com/mvj2ekht. Accessed on 15 December 2023.

launches.[38] The *New York Times* acknowledged in an article that with a success rate of almost 95 per cent, ISRO's rockets have halved the cost of satellite insurance, which has made India one of the most competitive launch sites in the world.[39]

In terms of cost, ISRO gives tough competition to Western agencies in the lucrative and growing international satellite launch market. Many countries now choose ISRO over other agencies in the developed world for satellite launches. Thus, criticizing ISRO helps the Western narrative in more than one way. It not only serves the commercial interests but also continues to reinforce the 'poor India' perception game.

---

[38]Sidharth M.P., 'ISRO Has Launched 397 Foreign Satellites in 10 Years Earning USD 441 Million', *WION News*, 15 December 2023, http://tinyurl.com/mx48jn6m. Accessed on 3 January 2024.

[39]Travelli, Alex, 'The Surprising Striver in the World's Space Business', *New York Times*, 4 July 2023, http://tinyurl.com/5929adsc. Accessed on 3 January 2024.

Chapter 5

COVID-19: A MODI-BASHING EVENT BY THE WESTERN MEDIA

When the Western media started writing about Covid-19 in India in early 2020, many of the reports also mentioned and referred to the Spanish Flu of the last century, which had wreaked havoc in the country. While a few mentioned it as a matter of fact, some stated that India could face the horrors of the Spanish Flu again as the country lacked necessary infrastructure to face the pandemic of Covid-19 proportions. Some foreign newspapers, while talking about the Spanish Flu, also mentioned that Mahatma Gandhi had also been caught in the grip of the deadly flu but somehow managed to survive.

Gulf News ran a story on 15 March 2020, titled 'How Spanish Flu Changed the Course of Indian History'. The story claimed, 'Mahatma Gandhi, the chief architect of India's independence, was one of the millions who contracted the Spanish flu. If he had not survived, India's struggle to shed the British colonial yoke would have taken a drastically different route.'[1]

A BBC India correspondent filed a story on the same lines on 18 March 2020, titled 'Coronavirus: What India Can Learn from the Deadly 1918 Flu'. The story claimed, 'The highly infectious Spanish flu had swept through the ashram in Gujarat where 48-year-old Gandhi was living, four years after he returned from South Africa.'[2] Gandhi and other ashram residents were lucky to recover, claimed the story.

Indian-language newspapers and online portals in India also joined in, and the content found space in many media publications. *Amar Ujala*, a prominent Hindi daily, did a story on 19 March 2020, claiming that Gandhi was infected with the Spanish Flu, which caused the death of crores of Indians.[3]

An Urdu newspaper, *The Siasat Daily*, filed a story a few months later on 2 July 2020, which stated that Gandhi had been infected with the Spanish Flu and that his daughter-in-law and her son had died.[4]

But did Gandhi actually catch the deadly Spanish Flu in

---

[1]Krishna, S.A., 'How the Spanish Flu Changed the Course of Indian History', *Gulf News*, 15 March 2020, http://tinyurl.com/5n6svw4s. Accessed on 29 December 2023.

[2]Biswas, Soutik, 'Coronavirus: What India Can Learn from the Deadly 1918 Flu', *BBC News*, 15 March 2020, http://tinyurl.com/4ju4y2an. Accessed on 29 December 2023.

[3]Sharma, S., 'वो जानलेवा वायरस, जिससे गांधी भी हो गए थे संक्रमित करोड़ों भारतीयों की हुई थी मौत', *Amar Ujala*, 19 March 2020, http://tinyurl.com/ycsh85ux. Accessed on 9 January 2024; Biswas, Soutik, 'Coronavirus: What India Can Learn from the Deadly 1918 Flu', *BBC News*, 15 March 2020, http://tinyurl.com/4ju4y2an. Accessed on 29 December 2023.

[4]Khan, S., 'Mahatma Gandhi Contracted Spanish Flu in 1918', *The Siasat Daily*, 2 July 2020, http://tinyurl.com/y4un7fwk. Accessed on 9 January 2024.

1918 as some media outlets reported during Covid-19?

GANDHI RUMOURED TO HAVE SPANISH FLU

It was in Gujarat in August 1918, when Gandhi was running a campaign to recruit Indians for the British Army during World War I, that he suffered his first long illness. This illness, which continued for months, was misconstrued as the Spanish Flu.

In early August 1918, Gandhi was already down with a bout of dysentery. On top of that, he had eaten the food that, according to him, did not suit his stomach. In his own words:

> There was some festival that day, and although I had to tell Kasturbai that I should have nothing for my midday meal, she tempted me and I succumbed. As I was under a vow of taking no milk products, she had prepared for me a sweet wheaten porridge with oil added to it instead of *ghi*. She had reserved too a bowlful of *mung* for me. I was fond of these things, and I really took them, hoping that without coming to grief I should eat just enough to please Kasturbai and to satisfy my palate. But the devil had been waiting for an opportunity. Instead of eating very little I had my fill of the meal. This was sufficient invitation to the angel of death. Within an hour the dysentery appeared in acute form.[5]

Around the same time, he further wrote:

---

[5]Gandhi, M.K., *My Experiments with Truth: An Autobiography,* Navajivan Publishing House, Ahmedabad, 1927, p. 551.

> The morning broke without death coming. But I could not get rid of the feeling that the end was near, and so I began to devote all my waking hours to listening to the Gita being read to me by the inmates of the Ashram. I was incapable of reading. I was hardly inclined to talk. The slightest talk meant a strain on the brain. All interest in living had ceased.[6]

At another place, Gandhi said, 'One night, I gave myself up to despair. I felt that I was at death's door. I sent word to Anasuyabehn. She ran down to the Ashram. Vallabhbhai [Patel] came up with Dr. Kanuga.'[7] The doctor told him that there was no danger to his life and that his pulse was fine. However, Gandhi did not believe the doctor as he was in unbearable pain.

The aforementioned utterances by Gandhi, which he had penned in his autobiography in 1927, are important to understand what had happened to him at that time. These words he expressed have given birth to a controversy over 90 years later.

Cycles of Half Truths

In 2017, Laura Spinney, a British health journalist, penned a book titled *Pale Rider: The Spanish Flu of 1918 and How It Changed the World*. Spinney's writings have appeared in prominent publications, including *National Geographic*, the *Economist*, and the *Telegraph*. In her book, she claimed that Gandhi's illness was not simply dysentery, but that he was infected with Spanish Flu. She writes in a very definitive

---

[6]Ibid. 554.

[7]Ibid. 553–4.

tone that 'Spanish flu—a gastric variety in his case—[...] incapacitated Gandhi at a critical moment in India's fight for independence'.[8] She concluded that the discontent generated from the devastation caused by the Spanish Flu in India catapulted Gandhi to be the undisputed leader of India's freedom movement.

An interview by Patt Morrison with Laura Spinney was published in the *Los Angeles Times* on 11 March 2020. Morrison, in her story, claimed that many world leaders, including the king of Spain, Mohandas K. Gandhi, Franklin D. Roosevelt and Walt Disney caught the virus but survived.[9]

Four days after the *Los Angeles Times* article, Morrison's by-line story based on the same content appeared in an opinion piece in the *Gulf News* on 15 March 2020.[10] A few hours later, the opinion editor of *Gulf News* wrote a piece based on the same Spinney and Morrison interview titled 'How the Spanish Flu Changed the Course of Indian History'.[11]

Gandhi's Take

In his autobiography, nowhere does Gandhi mention that he

[8]Spinney, Laura, *Pale Rider: The Spanish Flu of 1918 and How It Changed the World*, Jonathan Cape, London, 2017, p. 341.

[9]Morrison, P., 'What the Deadly 1918 Flu Epidemic Can Teach Us about Our Coronavirus Reaction', *Los Angeles Times,* 11 March 2020, http://tinyurl.com/y75xw6nh. Accessed on 9 January 2024.

[10]Morrison, P., 'What the Deadly 1918 Flu Epidemic Can Teach Us about Our Coronavirus Reaction', *Gulf News,* 15 March 2020, http://tinyurl.com/mu32h8f3. Accessed on 9 January 2024.

[11]Krishna, Shyam A., 'How the Spanish Flu Changed the Course of Indian History', *Gulf News,* 15 March 2020, http://tinyurl.com/5n6svw4s. Accessed on 9 January 2024.

contracted the Spanish Flu. He was always very meticulous in documenting what he did and was going through. He was a prolific writer and dictated letters and notes even when he was very sick.

Could it be the case that Gandhi did not realize that he had caught the virus? Could he have been ignorant of the fact that the world was reeling under a devastating pandemic and erroneously concluded that he only had a stomach ailment? These propositions are extremely unlikely.

Gandhi was well aware of the Spanish Flu greatly tormenting the world. This fact is evidenced by the various letters he wrote during that period.[12] One of them was to his eldest son Harilal, addressing the Spanish Flu afflicting his family.[13] He wrote another one to Reverend Charles Freer Andrews on learning that the latter had been suffering from the Spanish Flu.[14] In another letter to one of his lawyer friends, Gandhi speaks of the Spanish Flu and how it was impacting India.[15]

This is more than enough evidence of the fact that Gandhi was aware of the dangers of the Spanish Flu. He would have surely hinted if he had any suspicion of catching it during his long illness.

Instead, Gandhi's illness seems to have had roots in the physical and mental strain he had been under around that time. His efforts to recruit Indians for the British Army to

---

[12]Weber, Thomas and Dennis, 'Gandhi and the Pandemic', *Economic & Political Weekly*, 20 June 2020, http://tinyurl.com/y4bparey. Accessed on 9 January 2024.

[13]Gandhi, M.K., *The Collected Works of Mahatma Gandhi*, Volume 17, Publications Division, Government of India, New Delhi, 1999, p. 247.

[14]Ibid. 256.

[15]Ibid. 286.

fight World War I had resulted in physical exhaustion, and his work to placate the Muslim League and Ali brothers during Viceroyal war conferences—organized to seek cooperation of Indians in the War efforts and attended by Gandhi despite opposition from India's national leaders—had resulted in moral exhaustion. This combination proved too much for Gandhi's frail body and he fell ill.

Rajmohan Gandhi, one of Gandhi's grandsons who published his biography in 2006, mentioned the dilemma that his grandfather had faced. He states clearly in his biography that the illness was a result of extensive exhaustion: 'The heat, his failure with the peasants and above all, the clash between the recruiting activity and the nonviolence that he and close associates felt to be the message of his life... Exhausted in body, mind and soul, he had reached extremity.'[16]

One wonders where the issue of Gandhi being infected by the Spanish Flu virus popped up in 2020 and why it was being said during Covid-19 that he was infected with the Spanish Flu.

The timing of these stories is important. During the first phase of Covid-19, infections and deaths were rising alarmingly in the countries of Europe and the Americas. Cases had also slowly started showing an upward trend in parts of Asia, including India. Hence, there was an appetite for stories related to the present and past pandemics. Adding big names to pandemic stories made them catchy and sensational, which attracted more readers. Gandhi being infected with the Spanish Flu was definitely a story no network would like to miss. After all, it was a controversial story about India's biggest

---

[16]Gandhi, R., *Mohandas: A True Story of a Man, His People, and an Empire*, Penguin, New Delhi, 2006, p. 215.

leader during the freedom struggle. However, in the coverage, some more digging for the truth was expected, but no one bothered to check the sources that were readily available. Instead, Spinney's claims about Gandhi's illness became one of those social media forwards that keypad-happy netizens habitually sent to each other without giving a second thought to checking the authenticity of the information. Thus, one piece of misplaced information got multiplied by different networks, each competing not to be left behind.

SPANISH FLU AND COVID-19

It is true that Covid-19, which originated in the People's Republic of China, has been one of the gravest threats that humans have faced in the past few centuries. A comparable example of an outbreak of that magnitude in recent human memory is probably the Spanish Flu. That pandemic lasted for about two years, from March 1918 to March 1920, and is estimated to have killed 50–100 million people, which was around 2.5–5 per cent of the world population at that time. It surpassed the death count of World War I.[17] The first wave of the Spanish Flu was mild, and most deaths occurred during subsequent waves.[18] Meanwhile, the first case of Covid-19 in India was notified on 30 January 2020.[19] By January 2024, the total number of Covid-19 infections in the country stood at

---

[17]'WHO Director-General Addresses the Executive Board', *WHO*, 22 January 2018, http://tinyurl.com/4z77xd7z. Accessed on 9 January 2024.

[18]Ibid.

[19]Andrews, M.A., et al., 'First Confirmed Case of COVID-19 Infection in India: A Case Report', *Indian Journal of Medical Research*, Vol. 151, No. 5, May 2020, http://tinyurl.com/4rcsdn5f. Accessed on 12 January 2024.

44,483,502, with 533,409 reported deaths.[20] In comparison, the Spanish Flu of 1918 was estimated to have killed 10–20 million people in India.[21]

No effective vaccines or antiviral drugs were available to India in 1918. The world was also not that well connected then as it is today. With greater connectivity, there is more scientific collaboration and better coordinated research efforts. The global supply chains are more robust today than ever, and, hence, things reach from one corner of the word to the other very fast. But this has also given the virus wings to spread fast and wide. The duration of Covid-19 was the first time in human history when not one but many vaccines were developed and introduced as the pandemic was still ongoing. Suffice to say, since the Spanish Flu, things have changed considerably. Therefore, it is very problematic to draw parallels between Covid-19 and Spanish Flu as it may present a picture that is far removed from reality.

Unscientific Speculations

Published in the UK, the *Guardian* did a series of stories on Covid-19 in India. On 23 March 2020, it published an article titled 'The Virus Is Ravaging Rich Countries. What Happens When It Hits the Poor Ones?'[22] The article discussed the

---

[20]*Ministry of Health and Family Welfare, Government of India*, http://tinyurl.com/tzau2d4r. Accessed on 12 January 2024.

[21]Kant, Lalit and Guleria Randeep, 'Pandemic Flu, 1918: After Hundred Years, India Is as vulnerable', *Indian Journal of Medical Research*, Vol. 147, No. 3, March 2018, http://tinyurl.com/tbd3vp6b. Accessed on 12 January 2024.

[22]Malik, Nesrine, 'The Virus Is Ravaging Rich Countries. What Happens When It Hits the Poor Ones?', *Guardian*, 23 March 2020, https://tinyurl.com/mvkz6ftm. Accessed on 21 November 2023.

impact of Covid-19 in Africa. However, the writer almost compulsively mentions that 30 per cent of total Spanish Flu deaths in 1918–19 occurred in India. The article, along with the headline, almost predicted that developing countries like India were likely to get death counts as high as those during the Spanish Flu. It may be mentioned that when this report appeared the number of Covid-19 infections in India was only 499.[23] It was rather unscientific and illogical of the article to take a disease that is almost a century old and superimpose its outcome onto the present day, almost predicting the same results and thus creating unjustifiable panic. This kind of comparison is akin to fear mongering when published by mass media.

The *Guardian* followed up with a story a week later on 30 March 2020. The title of the story seems to have come out of a fictional series. This story, interestingly, is filed under a series called Global Development, which is supported by Bill and Melinda Gates Foundation. It reads, 'As the Wealthy Quaff Wine in Comfort, India's Poor Are Thrown to the Wolves.'[24]

The writer has attempted to exaggerate the economic disparity in India through the pandemic experience. They asserted that during the lockdown, while the poor struggled to survive, the rich lived their lives comfortably, without any significant disruption. Coming from a perspective of

---

[23]'Coronavirus in India: Covid-19 tally reaches 499, Domestic Flight Ops to Be Shut from March 25', *India Today,* 24 March 2020, http://tinyurl.com/hkdzz62y. Accessed on 9 January 2024.

[24]Dhillon, Amrit, 'As the Wealthy Quaff Wine in Comfort, India's Poor Are Thrown to the Wolves', *Guardian,* 30 March 2020, https://tinyurl.com/296wzdmf. Accessed on 21 November 2023.

being overly empathetic, the writer embellished the Indian poverty narrative, as most Western media does, in order to critique the lockdown. The writer added that the lives of millions of Indians were being shattered by the lockdown to an unimaginable degree, and the contrast between their suffering and the comfort of those who can ride out this storm is very sharp. The article only spoke in extremes by acknowledging the underprivileged and the über rich but did not provide an insight into the biggest economic segment of India—the middle classes—and the impact of lockdown on it.

Creating Doubts

As if on a mission to build a narrative, the *Guardian* published another story a day later, on 1 April 2020, where it cast doubts on the numbers shared by the experts. The story titled 'India Coronavirus Cases Rise amid Fears, True Figure Much Higher'[25] claimed that the actual number of Covid-19 infections in India was much higher than documented officially. The story stated that doubt had been cast over India's claim that it has no community transmission of Covid-19 after the country reported its biggest daily rise in number of cases so far, and connected it to a religious gathering held in Delhi two weeks prior.

Strangely, while the article quoted the officials for the above numbers, there was no expert quoted doubting these numbers. Then who was doubting those numbers? In such cases, if no expert has been quoted, it often means that the reporter or the

---

[25]Ellis-Petersen, Hannah, 'India Coronavirus Cases Rise amid Fears: True Figure Much Higher', *Guardian*, 1 April 2020, https://tinyurl.com/5n6cmkjk. Accessed on 21 November 2023.

newspaper is doubting the official numbers. Thus, it seemed to be simply the opinion of the writer without any facts.

Thrown under the Bus

On 8 April 2020, the *Guardian* published an opinion piece.[26] It talked of the lockdown and the movement of the migrant labourers. It compared the situation to Partition and quoted experts who believed that the lockdown was clamped by the Indian leadership in panic. It also claimed that India's Covid-19 response under the leadership of PM Narendra Modi had thrown common Indians 'under the bus'.

The opinion piece stated that the writer had discussed the Bengal famine of 1943, when about 3 million people had died, with Harsh Mander. The writer and Mander then went on to draw parallels with the situation then and now. Mander is quoted in the story saying that Covid-19 was another man-made crisis like the famine, and that the violence and the ongoing annihilation of the poor people could have been avoided had he been involved in the solution. How can these situations be compared when the Bengal famine killed over 3 million people, whereas the Covid-19 death toll in India is about half a million? The circumstances of both events were very different. Studies now say that the Bengal famine in 1943 was caused by the wrong policies of the then British PM Winston Churchill and not because of any drought.[27]

---

[26]Menezes, Vivek, 'India's Leaders Have Panicked. Now the Millions Who Power the Country Are Suffering', *Guardian*, 8 April 2020, http://tinyurl.com/y3yvajja. Accessed on 9 January 2024.

[27]Wilkinson, Bard, 'Churchill's Policies to Blame for Millions of Indian Famine Deaths, Study Says', *CNN*, 29 March 2019, http://tinyurl.com/2kef79c3. Accessed on 12 January 2024.

Thus, the famine was a man-made crisis, but Covid-19 was a pandemic that originated from China.

The *Guardian* article[28] seems politically motivated, with its uses of very strong phrases like 'annihilation of poor people', 'man-made crisis', etc., and this is evidenced by its praise for measures against Covid-19 by only two state governments, those of Kerala and Maharashtra. These states were ruled by parties that were in Opposition at the centre. Kerala was ruled by the Communist Party of India (Marxist) (CPM) and Maharashtra was ruled by a coalition of Shiv Sena, the Congress Party and the Nationalist Congress Party—all of them were opposed to the Narendra Modi-led government.

To say that only these two states fared much better than others in terms of Covid-19 management is far from the truth. In fact, an attempt at a narrative in the initial days of Covid-19 infections was made by a section of the media to prove that the 'Kerala Model' was the best model and that it was successful in stopping infections from spreading.[29] Many stories lauding the so-called Kerala Model appeared in some international publications. It actually proved to be just a propaganda tool, as later the number of cases in Kerala rose significantly faster than other states.[30] An *Indian Express* report stated that the initial stories praising the Kerala model were more of a PR exercise. Thus, the series of articles

[28]Ibid.

[29]Masih, Niha, 'Aggressive Testing, Contact Tracing, Cooked Meals: How the Indian State of Kerala Flattened Its Coronavirus Curve', *Washington Post,* 13 April 2020, http://tinyurl.com/44ss7cj5. Accessed on 9 January 2024.

[30]Joseph, Anoop Antony, 'Why "Kerala Model" of Failed Covid Handling Should Learn from UP', *Indian Express,* 18 August 2021, http://tinyurl.com/3y293x8m. Accessed on 9 January 2024.

published in the newspaper were part of a campaign not based on facts. It was as if the paper wanted to say that the Modi government was responsible for Covid-19 and its impact on India. This claim was far from the truth. In any case, it was unnecessary to single out two states for their good work, only based on political leanings. It gave the impression of vilifying the ruling parties in other states of the country. This was a clear example of baseless partisanship.

∽

During Covid-19, an influential section of the European and US English media started to build a commentary around India that was essentially negative in tone, tenor and intent. It possibly came out of the ideological belief that nothing right could be done in India, especially by the government led by PM Narendra Modi. The prominent Western media declared that this 'Hindu nationalist government' was incapable of fighting the virus. It treated India's efforts to combat the pandemic with disdain, but its conspicuous efforts to undermine this government's efforts in abating the situation drew flak from many eminent people. Ramesh Rao, professor of communications at the Columbus State University, Georgia, USA, stated, 'Since the Bharatiya Janata Party (BJP) came to power in 2014, with Narendra Modi elected as the Prime Minister, the thumping of war drums in these newspapers and magazines, as well as on radio and TV, has been continuous. [...] the BJP [is] labelled and identified as a "Hindu nationalist party", and Modi characterized as a chest-thumping Hindu hegemon [...].'[31]

---

[31]Rao, Ramesh, 'The New York Times' Prejudiced Gaze at India, Hindus,

Even a cursory reading of the headlines about India, which were produced by the Western media in the first 15 months of the pandemic, from March 2020 to May 2021, had a truly astounding result. As part of research for this book, the coverage of the *Telegraph*, the *Guardian*, *BBC News*, the *Washington Post*, the *New York Times*, the *Wall Street Journal*, the *Independent* and *Time* was observed. A collection of 230 news stories from India related to Covid-19 were shortlisted from the articles published by these newspapers during the first two waves of Covid-19 in India. These were then analysed in detail. The simple random sample method was used to select the articles. After the sampling, items were searched to use keywords related to Covid-19 and India. The articles selected pertained to Covid-19, and issues and events related to it. These included lockdown, vaccine, death, migrant workers, travel, economy, mass funerals, diplomacy and medicine, among others.

Majority of these news stories were opinion pieces or articles written by invited columnists. Actual ground reporting for these was limited to about less than one-fourth of the articles. More than three-fourths of the news items discussed focussed on the actions of the central government and the Indian PM. Most of them were critical of both.

While there is no harm in criticizing the government if the critique is fact-based, logical and gives appropriate space to the opposing viewpoints, it was not the case with the coverage by these international publications. These articles were mostly one-sided, the experts chosen were generally

---

Hinduism', *IndiaChapter.in*, http://tinyurl.com/2p9uabuh. Accessed on 9 January 2024.

those who were known ideological critics of the government and majority of the opinion-piece writers also belonged to this category.

RELIGIOUS OVERTONES

Though the overriding theme was Covid-19, among the news websites of these publications, many of the items had religious or communal overtones. The communal issues were brought in when it was not necessary to do so. The religious festivals belonging to the majority Hindu community were generally described in a manner that indicated that these could result in a spread of infections. Speculations of the possibility of Diwali, Onam or Rakhi celebrations further spreading the virus were prominently featured. Multiple articles came out fearing Kumbh Mela becoming a hotspot for the dreaded disease. These have been mentioned in the Annexure.

According to a discussion in Parliament in July 2023, India has one of the largest Muslim population, with around 200 million Muslims as its citizens.[32] Approximately 27.8 million Indians are Christian by faith according to the 2011 Census (a proximate of the number of Christians in India in 2023 is unavailable). Fairness required that all festivals—whether Hindu, Islamic, Christian or others—were treated as being on the same footing. However, some of the publications chose to ignore festivals other than those belonging to the Hindu community while linking these to incidents of Covid-19. This

[32]According to the 2011 census, the Muslim population in India was around 172.2 million.

appeared as a partisan and communal approach to a problem that was essentially an international health crisis.

FLOATING UNAUTHENTICATED INFORMATION

Sourcing is an important part of any story. Credible and known sources can provide authenticity to a story. In the shortlisted news stories by Western media about Covid-19 in India, around two-thirds of the sources quoted were not established or known. Many of the items were based on self-assessment or on *vox populi*. Many times, little-known NGOs were quoted, but the government or official version was generally not given space, even though the Supreme Court of India had directed the media to carry the official version while reporting on Covid-19.

On 31 March 2020, the Supreme Court of India noted that the migration of labourers working in the cities to their home in large numbers was triggered by panic created by news that the lockdown would continue for more than three months. The Court observed[33] that it was not possible for it to overlook the menace of fake news by electronic, print or social media because the panic-driven migration caused great deal of problems to those who acted on such news, causing some to even lose their lives.[34] It further said, 'We expect the media (print, electronic or social) to maintain a strong sense of responsibility and ensure that unverified

[33] *Alakh Alok Srivastava vs. Union of India*, W.P.(C) No. 468 of 2020, http://tinyurl.com/fvk3xxru. Accessed on 19 January 2024.

[34] 'Supreme Court Concerned over "Fake News" on Covid-19', *Hindustan Times*, 1 April 2020, http://tinyurl.com/mrx4dcda. Accessed on 9 January 2024.

news capable of causing panic is not disseminated. We do not intend to interfere with the free discussion about the pandemic, but direct the media to refer to and publish the official version about the developments.'[35]

Despite the clear directions of the Supreme Court of India on Covid-19 reporting, most US and European media mostly continued to report based on lopsided information. Very often, they did not even quote the official version of the Covid-19-related developments in India. They used the information that suited their narrative. One example of this is when Sanjeev Sanyal, then principal economic advisor to the finance minister, was interviewed by the *New York Times* for 40 minutes but only two words by him were used in the story that was published.[36] The paper instead chose to describe the Shramik Special trains to ferry labourers during the early months of Covid-19 home as 'Virus Trains'.[37] Sanyal later shared the entire interview on an *X* thread.[38] The article wanted to push a pre-decided narrative, and, possibly, the Sanyal interview did not suit it, so it decided to use only two words from the lengthy conversation. '30 of 40 mins was

---

[35]'Don't Disseminate Unverified News Capable of Causing Panic: SC to Media', *Press Information Bureau,* 1 April 2020, http://tinyurl.com/yhthxfnc. Accessed on 9 January 2024.

[36]Sharma, Nupur J., 'How the New York Times Reduced a 40-Minute Conversation with Sanjeev Sanyal to Merely 2 Words to Prove that Shramik Trains Were "Virus Trains"', *OpIndia,* 16 December 2020, http://tinyurl.com/yc6bhb4r. Accessed on 9 January 2024.

[37]Gettleman, Jeffery, et al., 'The Virus Trains: How Lockdown Chaos Spread Covid-19 Across India', *New York Times,* 15 December 2020, http://tinyurl.com/mfr6cyzc. Accessed on 9 January 2024.

[38]@sanjeevsanyal, *X* (formerly Twitter), 16 December 2020, 11.19 a.m., http://tinyurl.com/2j7sfhad. Accessed on 9 January 2024.

about the thinking behind India's policy response. As will be obvious, the journalist was not interested. She already had an agenda to push a pre-decided story,' wrote Sanyal in his tweet.

RELATING THE UNRELATED

On 5 May 2020, the *Guardian* published an opinion related to the pandemic under the headline, 'Where India's Government Has Failed in the Pandemic, Its People Have Stepped In.'[39] Prima facie, on reading the headline, it seems that the Covid-19 situation had become terrible in India, while the reality was totally different. On that particular day, India had reported only 3,900 positive cases. On the other hand, the USA and the UK had reported 29,266 and 3,985 positive cases, respectively.[40] One can see that the USA, with less than one-fourth the population of India, had 7.5 times more Covid-19 cases than India. Even the UK had more cases per million than India when the former's population is at least 20 times less than that of the latter.

The opinion also criticized the Indian government's decisions to ban certain NGOs in India and implied that the ban hindered Covid-19-related social work. Contrary to the article's claim, the GoI had not cancelled the licences to receive foreign funds of over 20,000 NGOs. Nityanand Rai, the minister of state in the Ministry of Home Affairs,

---

[39]Ramachandran, Bharati, 'Where India's Government Has Failed in the Pandemic, Its People Have Stepped In', *Guardian*, 5 May 2020, http://tinyurl.com/23zu4pyw. Accessed on 9 January 2024.

[40]*Coronavirus disease (COVID-19): Situation Report* – 106, WHO, http://tinyurl.com/mrymj4k5. Accessed on 9 January 2024.

disclosed the official figures in Rajya Sabha: 'Registration certificates of approximately 14,500 associations have been cancelled during the last five years.'[41]

The cited reasons for cancellation of licences included the NGOs misutilizating their funds and not submitting their annual returns on time. Without even going into the merits of the reasons cited for the cancellations of licences of the NGOs, one can safely say that the opinion piece was wrong in connecting the Covid-19-related work and the act of cancellations by the GoI. There is a huge time gap between the cancellation and Covid-19.

While the reason for cancellation was non-adherence to Indian laws, the opinion tried to mislead its readers by combining it with Covid-19-related activities. There was no correlation between the cancellation of NGO licences and Covid-19 relief work. The cancellation happened after 2014 when the Modi government came to power. Clearly, it was much before Covid-19 hit India in 2020. The question to ponder here is: does this not amount to building a fake narrative? The newspaper showed a particular penchant for sensationalizing the Covid-19 news in India, by erroneously spicing it with other events.

LINKING CHILD LABOUR WITH COVID-19

'Covid-19 Prompts "Enormous Rise" in Demand for Cheap Child Labour in India'—this news was published by the

---

[41]Rajya Sabha Secretariat, *Parliamentary Debates Rajya Sabha Official Report (Floor Version)*, Vol. 250, No. 13, 4 December 2019, http://tinyurl.com/3yxtjn8a. Accessed on 22 January 2024.

Guardian on 13 October 2020.[42] According to the website, after the lockdown imposed due to the pandemic, crimes against children started increasing across the country. In this context, an example of 70 children allegedly being taken for wages from Bihar to Rajasthan was given. Apart from this, comments of some Indian NGOs were also included to make the story look convincing. The article looked incomplete as it did not mention the city the children were rescued in or a mention of a first information report (FIR).

It also claimed that children of poor families in India were forced to work as the families had nothing to eat, but this seemed to be aimed at dramatizing India's poverty and creating an impression of administrative failure more than stating facts. It did not account for the free ration that was being provided by the government to poor families.[43]

Just few days before the *Guardian* story, Union Labour Minister Santosh Gangwar had already commented on the worry about increased levels of child labour during the pandemic and 'called for suitable action in this regard,'[44] but his statement was not mentioned in the article.

The intention of the article comes across as trying to create a sensational link between child labour and the pandemic without examining the situation holistically.

---

[42]Ellis-Petersen, Hannah and Manoj Chaurasia, 'Covid-19 Prompts "Enormous Rise" in Demand for Cheap Child Labour in India,' *Guardian*, 13 October 2020, http://tinyurl.com/yuype5p5. Accessed on 9 January 2024.

[43]Tiwary, Deeptiman, 'Poor Hardest Hit, PM Extends Free rations until November,' *Indian Express,* 1 July 2020, http://tinyurl.com/ydxxpjjy. Accessed on 12 December 2023.

[44]PTI, 'Ending Child Labour Is a Priority of the Government, Says Santosh Gangwar,' *Times of India,* 9 October 2020, http://tinyurl.com/yfm7csbv. Accessed on 9 January 2024.

COVID-19 DEATHS AND THE NEW YORK TIMES

During the pandemic, the *New York Times* seemed like it was on a fishing expedition to prove that the Modi government could do nothing right during the pandemic. Criticizing the government at every turn for sensationalism seemed to be a key action of the reports published in the Western newspapers during the period. The *New York Times* did a story in April 2021 where it had started its campaign to doubt India's official Covid-19 numbers. The story was titled 'As Covid-19 Devastates India, Deaths Go Undercounted.'[45]

This was followed by a story on 25 May 2021 titled 'Just How Big Could India's Covid Toll Be.'[46] The story, based on the premise that the official figures were underreported, estimated that in the worst case scenario, more than 700 million Indians, which was over half of the country's population, could have been infected by the virus and 4.2 million Indians could have died of Covid-19 by 25 May 2021. To put things in perspective, the total number of infections in the entire world till June 2023 is estimated to be around 689 million.[47] This number is decidedly less than the number estimated for India in 2021. There were 307,231 Covid-19 deaths reported in India till the day the report was published, while the likely estimate by the *New*

---

[45]Gettleman, Jeffery, et al., 'As Covid-19 Devastates India, Deaths Go Undercounted', *New York Times,* 24 April 2021, http://tinyurl.com/49kwh8ue. Accessed on 9 January 2024.

[46]Gamio, Lazaro and James Glanz, 'Just How Big Could India's Covid Toll Be?', *New York Times,* 25 May 2021, http://tinyurl.com/3j32j7cp. Accessed on 3 January 2024.

[47]http://tinyurl.com/buhppr2n. Accessed on 7 June 2023.

York Times in the worst case scenario was of 4.2 million. The total Covid-19 mortality in India in January 2024 was 533,412.[48] The total number of Covid-19-related deaths the world over in May 2021 stood at 3,519,307 as per the World Health Organization (WHO) estimates.[49] So, the *New York Times*'s worst-case fatality projections for India surpassed the total death numbers for the entire world. It didn't even make any mathematical sense. This seems completely outrageous.

The *New York Times* followed up this story again in July 2021.[50] But this time, it was generous enough to bring down the likely Covid-19 deaths in India to over 3 million. This was again a speculative story that quoted a report by the Washington-based think tank called Global Development Centre, not taking into account the official data. One understands that media and journalists need to question things, but this obsession on proving that the official casualty figures were wrong in India seems to have gone too far.

The GoI called the *New York Times* report 'totally baseless and absolutely false'.[51] It said that the report was ad hoc and was based on wrong assumptions without any evidence. A look at the Covid-19 numbers in 2023 indeed

---

[48]Ibid.

[49]'COVID-19 Situation Updates for Week 21 (23–29 May 2021)', *WHO*, http://tinyurl.com/4buxsdn8. Accessed on 9 January 2024.

[50]Singh, Karan Deep, 'India's True Pandemic Death Toll Is Likely to Be Well Over 3 Million, a New Study Finds', *New York Times*, 20 July 2021, http://tinyurl.com/3fd8zj3k. Accessed on 9 January 2024.

[51]'NYT Report on India Covid Toll "Absolutely False", Says Government', *Times of India*, 28 May 2021, http://tinyurl.com/bdcrn5ew. Accessed on 9 January 2024.

makes it clear that the *New York Times* was completely wrong in its estimations of Covid-19-related deaths in India. The comparative numbers establish that India has done much better than the developed world.

Covid-19 Numbers: India and the Developed World

The figures given below depict a different pattern from what the Western media reported. India, with the largest population base, fared much better. If we consider Covid-19 deaths per million of total population, the numbers are very stark. As per Table 1, the mortality rate per million of population in France is 2,553, the UK is 3,303, Germany is 2,078, Italy is 3,161, Russia is 2,738, the US is 3,483 and Brazil is 3,266. The Covid-19 deaths per million of population in India is only 378.

Table 1: Comparative Covid-19 Numbers (January 2024).

Country	*Total population*	*Total number of reported infections*	*Total deaths*	*Total cases per million of population*	*Total deaths per million of population*
USA	334,805,269	110,495,095	1,191,861	330,028	3,560
France	65,584,518	40,138,560	167,642	612,013	2,556
UK	68,497,907	24,812,582	232,112	362,239	3,389
Germany	83,883,596	38,791,727	181,044	462,447	2,158
Italy	60,262,770	26,692,251	195,494	442,931	3,244
Russia	145,805,947	23,798,457	401,543	163,220	2,754
Brazil	215,353,593	38,230,814	708,739	177,526	3,291
India	**1,406,631,776**	**45,021,383**	**533,412**	**32,007**	**379**

Source: http://tinyurl.com/buhppr2n. Accessed on 14 January 2024.

The New York Times at War with Itself

Obviously, these numbers do not suit the narrative that the Western press had been building about Covid-19 in India. Surprisingly, the *New York Times*'s June 2023 Covid-19 data acknowledged total deaths in India to be 530,779.[52] The article stated that over 70 per cent of Indians were vaccinated, and it also showed that the deaths per one lakh people in India were only 39. If the June 2023 *New York Times* data is true, which seems to be the case, then should the paper and its editors not have tendered an open and unconditional apology to the people of India for its earlier exaggerated predictions?

In all fairness, the paper should have come out and said that it was wrong in publishing previous stories as they had got their facts wrong. Decency, journalistic ethics, professionalism, honesty and truthfulness demand it. Surely the people of India deserve this from the *New York Times*. However, it is not sure that the publication is brave and transparent enough to admit its mistakes. And, therefore it is safe to presume that the paper was on an agenda-driven campaign against the government and people of India when the Covid-19 was at its peak.

INDIAN VACCINES AND DISCRIMINATION BY BRITISH GOVERNMENT

Indians planning to travel to the UK were baffled when the UK government announced the new Covid-19 travel guidelines on 17 September 2021. As per these guidelines,

[52]'Coronavirus World Map: Tracking the Global Outbreak,' *New York Times*, 10 March 2023, http://tinyurl.com/3vk97hbj. Accessed on 8 June 2023.

vaccinated Indians were to be treated as unvaccinated and had to be compulsorily quarantined. It was the time when the initial waves of the pandemic had abated and the world was trying to open up. Indians and citizens of some other Third-World countries were unfairly burdened with the Covid-19-related travel protocol, whereas citizens from developed countries were given different status.[53] This move shocked the Indian government, as it was against the declared policies and announcements by the British government up till then. These rules, announced by the UK's transport secretary, Grant Shapps, were to be effective from 4 October 2021.[54] Under the new rules, travellers fully vaccinated with Oxford/AstraZeneca, Pfizer/BioNTech, Moderna or Janssen shots in the USA, Australia, New Zealand, South Korea or any EU country were to be considered 'fully vaccinated' and exempt from quarantine when they arrived in England from an amber-list country. However, people who had been vaccinated with the similar vaccines in many countries in Africa and Latin America, as well as other countries, including India, were termed as 'not fully vaccinated' and were forced to quarantine for 10 days on arrival. They were to undergo mandatory Covid-19 tests, which were expensive. The revised UK guidelines had approved the Indian Covishield vaccine. However, the list of countries whose citizens were allowed to skip the quarantine

---

[53]Ghosh, D., 'Problem Isn't Covishield But India's Vaccine Certificate, Says UK', *India News*, 21 September 2021, http://tinyurl.com/5cjbs663. Accessed on 9 January 2024.

[54]Quinn, Ben and Peter Walker, 'What Are the Changes to Covid Rules for International Travel?', *Guardian*, 17 September 2021, http://tinyurl.com/mttfjk8f. Accessed on 9 January 2024.

and Covid-19 tests did not include India.[55]

The Covishield vaccine was produced in India under licence from AstraZeneca by the Serum Research Institute of India.[56] The same vaccines were exported to many UN entities and to 95 countries in the world, including the UK, and were found acceptable.[57] The list also included Canada, New Zealand, Australia and the Netherlands. Citizens of these countries did not need to quarantine upon arrival in the UK. The fact is that in March 2021, the UK government had imported 5 million doses of the vaccine from the very same institute.[58] It meant that the UK citizens who were inoculated with the imported Indian vaccine were considered 'vaccinated', while Indians who also got the same vaccine were considered unsafe, indicating discrimination against Indian travellers. The UK government attributed this to issues regarding certification, India's CoWIN app and the authenticity of Indian data.

Speculative stories based on hearsay were fed to the media regarding these. When asked, the British High Commissioner to India, Alex Ellis CMG, said, 'India is still on the Amber category because there are still some COVID-19 cases in India. Most other nations on the list that do not need any quarantine are in the green category, where the

---

[55]Sinha, Saurabh, 'UK Accepts Covishield, but Indians to Quarantine', *Times of India*, 23 Sepember 2021, http://tinyurl.com/2ncttsyx. Accessed on 9 January 2024.

[56]Srivatsan, K.C., 'Covishield: A Timeline of the Covid-19 Vaccine Manufactured by Serum Institute of India', *Hindustan Times*, 16 January 2021, http://tinyurl.com/ysvp2smm. Accessed on 6 December 2023.

[57]'Vaccine Supply', *Ministry of External Affairs, Government of India*, http://tinyurl.com/y2345bac. Accessed on 9 January 2024.

[58]Ibid.

number of active cases is very low in comparison.' He further said that while the Covishield vaccine was approved, the UK authorities were still trying to understand the working of India's CoWIN app. He added that his government was letting the Indian government understand the working of the UK Covid app, and that once the UK was satisfied, it would remove quarantine conditions for Indian travellers.[59]

His other argument was that the countries whose citizens need not quarantine were those 'where the number of active cases are very low in comparison' to India.[60] However, this was factually incorrect. Back then, the number of active cases was much higher in the USA, for example, as compared to India. By this logic, the Americans should also have been on the list of travellers needing quarantine. The fact is that the number of active cases in the UK was higher than India. Thus, it can be discerned that the policy was discriminatory and possibly was decided looking at the colour of the passport rather than being based on facts.

BBC Withholds Information

A BBC report on the UK announcement is intriguing. Dated 22 September 2021, the report, headlined 'Covishield: UK Recognises Covid Jab after India Outcry', narrated that India was enraged because people found the Covid-19 travel policy discriminatory.[61] It went on to present Indian leadership's

---

[59]Ghosh, D., 'Problem Isn't Covishield But India's Vaccine Certificate, Says UK', *India News*, 21 September 2021, http://tinyurl.com/5cjbs663. Accessed on 9 January 2024.

[60]Ibid.

[61]Biswas, S., 'Covishield: UK Recognises Covid Jab after India Outcry', *BBC News,* 22 September 2021, http://tinyurl.com/25hnazuu. Accessed on 9

reaction, among other things. However, the story makes for a very interesting read. The report seems to have been written in a manner to justify the British government's announcement. The BBC report raises doubts regarding fake vaccines and states that WHO had reported that authorities had seized such vaccines in Africa and India between July and August 2021. The story also tried to create doubts about the documentation related to the Indian vaccination programme. The report called it 'dodgy documentation'.

The issue of fake vaccines in circulation had come to notice a month before this report was published. The government officials had assured that no Indian had been inoculated with a fake vaccine.[62] It may also be noted that it was the Indian surveillance system that alerted about the possibility of such counterfeit vaccines.

The BBC report also cited a report of a US-based cybersecurity company called Check Point.[63] It stated that the Check Point research had discovered that there was a surging black market in vaccine certificates on the messaging app Telegram in 28 countries. It said that these certificates were sold for $75 in India.

What the BBC story failed to disclose was that the original company study mentioned 28 countries, which also included the UK and the USA. The allusion that the

---

January 2024.

[62]Sharma, Neetu Chandra, 'WHO Issues Medical Alert on Fake Covishield Vaccines', *Mint,* 18 August 2021, http://tinyurl.com/bd669ac5. Accessed on 9 January 2024.

[63]*Your Checkpoint : Threat Intelligence Report,* Check Point Research, 13–19 September 2021, p. 1, http://tinyurl.com/mpcd3cj3. Accessed on 9 January 2024.

regulations excluded Indian citizens because of the problem of fake certification in India holds no water because this problem, as per the Check Point report, was as much in the USA and UK as in India. This one-sided interpretation of data in the Check Point report by the BBC needs to be looked at to realize that India and Western countries are not treated equally by the Western media.

The controversy regarding the British Covid-19 policy against travellers from India continued for about 20 days, after which the Modi government imposed the same restrictions on British citizens on the principle of reciprocity. The British government then wilted under this diplomatic pressure (as opposed to realizing the error of its ways), and vaccinated Indian travellers were finally treated at par with those from developed countries.[64]

CALLING DELTA VARIANT AS INDIAN VARIANT

Calling the most devastating strain of Covid-19 the 'Indian variant' instead of 'Delta variant' was a campaign to sully the name of the country. A BBC story filed on 19 May 2021 was headlined 'India Variant: Why Was India Not Put on the Red List Sooner?'[65] Another story by the broadcaster said that three cases of 'Indian variant' were found in Leicester.[66] The

---

[64]Sibal, Sidhant, 'Tit-for-Tat: 10-Day Quarantine Must for All UK Travellers to India, Despite Vaccination', *Zee News,* 1 October 2021, https://tinyurl.com/5ab7ssha. Accessed on 6 December 2023.

[65]Reality Check Team, 'India Variant: Why Was India Not Put on the Red List Sooner?', *BBC News,* 19 May 2021, http://tinyurl.com/4pkxbphs. Accessed on 9 January 2024.

[66]'Covid: Three Cases of Indian Variant Found in Leicester', *BBC News,* 28 April 2021, http://tinyurl.com/y5a9b3vj. Accessed on 9 January 2024.

BBC used this name in many of its stories. The *Telegraph*, too, in a story dated 27 May 2021, covered a story that stated that the number of cases infected with the 'Indian variant' in the UK had doubled in a week.[67] Similar nomenclature of that particular strain of Covid-19 was used in stories by the *Guardian, Daily Mail, Mirror, Reuters, Al Jazeera, Wall Street Journal,* etc. It is important to recall that neither WHO, nor any other body had described the Delta variant as the 'Indian variant'. A pertinent question to ask here is: did the media call the first Covid-19 strain the Chinese variant as it came from Wuhan? No. So, why was there a need to describe the strain originating in India as 'Indian variant'? This was a crude attempt to defame a country.[68]

Even though the USA was one of the worst affected nations, it did not have a variant named after it. The Alpha variant, B.1.1.7, which was spotted in the UK in September 2020, was not called the UK variant by the press either.[69] Then why was a variant called 'Indian variant'? Interestingly, after India objected, WHO named the two variants originating in India as 'Kappa' and 'Delta'.[70]

The entire campaign had a geopolitical angle as well. The geopolitical and strategic landscape in Asia in general and in India's immediate neighbourhood in particular had been going through a fundamental shift even before the Covid-19

---

[67]McTaggart, India and Gareth Davies, 'Indian Variant Now Comprises Up to Three-Quarters of New Cases, Matt Hancock Warned', *Telegraph,* 27 May 2021, http://tinyurl.com/2ph97j43. Accessed on 9 January 2024.

[68]'WHO Labels India, Other Global Covid Variants with Greek Names. Check Full List Here', *Mint,* 5 June 2021, http://tinyurl.com/2s3mhh9s. Accessed on 9 January 2024.

[69]Ibid.

[70]Ibid.

disaster was unleashed on the world. India and China had been competing for influence in this ongoing geostrategic upheaval in the aftermath of the USA's diminishing role in the region. Covid-19 hastened this process. On one hand, PM Modi's 'Neighbourhood First' doctrine and his sustained outreach to the Gulf countries need to be seen from this perspective.[71] On the other hand, Chinese strongman Xi Jinping's Belt and Road Initiative was also a policy to broaden communist China's sphere of influence much beyond its borders.

VACCINE DIPLOMACY AND GEOPOLITICS OF THE PANDEMIC

The Covid-19 outbreak, which was fundamentally a human health tragedy, soon turned into a political tussle between the USA and China. The media on both sides became a handy tool to carry out propaganda. The USA blamed China for the origin of the pandemic. Then US President Donald Trump and Secretary of State Mike Pompeo alleged that the virus originated from a lab in Wuhan.[72] The *Washington Post* article titled 'In Search for Coronavirus Origin, Hubei Caves and Wildlife Farms Draw New Scrutiny' also indicated that it came from China.[73] However, China rebutted these

---

[71]Pattanaik, Smruti S., 'India's "Neighbourhood First" Policy', *Background Note on India's 'Neighbourhood First' Policy,* Lok Sabha Secretariat, New Delhi, 2022, http://tinyurl.com/34devmt5. Accessed on 9 January 2024.

[72]Gan, Nectar, 'The Wuhan Lab at the Center of the US-China Blame Game: What We Know and What We Don't', *CNN,* 6 May 2020, http://tinyurl.com/mr4bzzwd. Accessed on 9 January 2024.

[73]Standaert, Michael and Eva Dou, 'In Search for Coronavirus Origins, Hubei Caves and Wildlife Farms Draw New Scrutiny', *Washington Post,* 11 October

allegations. The influential Chinese English daily, the *Global Times*, in an article titled 'Covid 19 Likely in US before Wuhan; World Should Not Turn Blind Eye to Similar Cases', claimed that the first Covid-19 case may have originated in the USA.[74] The paper later claimed that the virus came from an US Army facility.[75]

Soon, it turned into an international power tussle, and WHO became a casualty, with the USA accusing the organization of having become a 'puppet of China'.[76] It then withdrew from WHO. There are a number of conspiracy theories in the Western- and Chinese-supported media along similar lines. Many Western publications wrote about the India and China rivalry as well. For example, the BBC wrote that China had weakened in its global positioning and outreach in the wake of the pandemic and that India was trying to take that space.[77] As the world was battling the pandemic, Covid-19 became a part of international diplomatic struggle for countries to exert and increase influence in the world.

Health diplomacy became a focal point of foreign policy

2021, http://tinyurl.com/mvtxam8b. Accessed on 9 January 2024.

[74]Liu Caiyu and Fan Lingzhi, 'COVID-19 Likely in US before Wuhan; World Should Not Turn a Blind Eye to Similar Cases: Experts', *Global Times*, 2 December 2020, http://tinyurl.com/2mtrrefv. Accessed on 9 January 2024.

[75]Xin Ping, 'The US Still Owes the World an Explanation on COVID-19 Origins Tracing', *Global Times*, 28 June 2022, http://tinyurl.com/5n725ktj. Accessed on 9 January 2024.

[76]Hinshaw, Drew, 'Trump Moves to Pull U.S. out of World Health Organization in Midst of Covid-19 Pandemic', *Wall Street Journal*, 7 July 2020, http://tinyurl.com/3rn33tzy. Accessed on 9 January 2024.

[77]Inamdar, Nikhil, 'Coronavirus: Can India Replace China as World's Factory?', *BBC News*, 18 May 2020, http://tinyurl.com/ykbrnp9j. Accessed on 9 January 2024.

for many countries, including India. In any case, India was considered the 'pharmacy of the world'.[78] Its pharma exports have been rising in the last decade. During the pandemic, India started to reach out to many countries in the world to provide medicines and other materials. The philosophy of *vasudhaiva kutumbakam* (the whole world is my family) is an intrinsic part of India's civilizational ethos since the ancient times.

India's efforts to help the international community have been captured well in a research article published in the *Journal of Asian and African Studies*.[79] It stated that during the pandemic, around half-a-dozen Indian firms worked with the USA, the UK and Russian pharmaceutical companies. It also credited India with developing vaccines against Covid-19. India had been producing 1.5 billion doses of different vaccines annually. Doses of 20 such vaccines were being exported to 165 countries. The research article recognized that India had developed a 'live-attenuated' vaccine for Covid-19 in collaboration with an American biotech company. India also exported massive consignments of hydroxychloroquine, a drug that was in demand in an earlier phase of the pandemic. Paracetamol tablets were also supplied to at least 100 countries. The report also compliments India for delivering hydroxychloroquine and paracetamol tablets to the Gulf Cooperation Council (GCC) countries.[80]

---

[78]Masurkar, Nikkhil S., 'Why Is India the Pharmacy of the World?', *Financial Express*, 25 September 2021, http://tinyurl.com/ydnt579h. Accessed on 9 January 2024.

[79]Singh, Bawa, et al., 'India's Neighbourhood Vaccine Diplomacy During COVID-19 Pandemic: Humanitarian and Geopolitical Perspectives', *Journal of Asian and African Studies*, Volume 58, No. 6, http://tinyurl.com/4ra7wku3. Accessed on 9 January 2024.

[80]Ibid.

India's Indigenous Vaccine Programme and Pharma Lobby

Under the programme Vaccine Maitri, India supplied vaccines to several countries.[81] Two lobbies were unnerved with the success of this humanitarian initiative. One was based in China and the other was the powerful international pharma lobby, which happens to be based in Western countries.[82]

This humanitarian initiative by India was questioned by the Western media. Some media reports described it as unsustainable. The *Guardian* published an article titled 'The World's Poorest Countries Are at India's Mercy for Vaccines. It's Unsustainable' in April 2021, stating that India should have exported 50 per cent of the vaccines produced by the Serum Research Institute.[83] It may be noted that this was being said at a time when only 3 per cent of Indians were vaccinated. The country had exported a number of vaccines earlier, but it had stopped the exports when the deadly second wave of the pandemic hit the country. The article lamented that India had not spent any money on research and development of the vaccines. The article seemed to be soft on the Western pharma lobby and rationalized its refusal to give vaccines to other countries by claiming that the Western pharmaceutical industry was not in a position

---

[81]'Vaccine Maitri', *Ministry of External Affairs,* http://tinyurl.com/3f4wvcum. Accessed on 9 January 2024.

[82]Agarwal, Gopal Krishna, 'Is the Global Pharma Industry Unhappy with India's Policies?', *Hindustan Times,* 10 June 2021, http://tinyurl.com/5fu8huw6. Accessed on 9 January 2024.

[83]Prabhala, Achal and Leena Menghaney, 'The World's Poorest Countries Are at India's Mercy for Vaccines. It's Unsustainable', *Guardian,* 2 April 2021, http://tinyurl.com/4duwxku4. Accessed on 9 January 2024.

to supply vaccines outside Western countries.

On one hand, India was targeted by the Western media; on the other, China started a smear campaign against India's outreach to poorer countries of the Global South to target India's health diplomacy initiative. An analysis of the situation by Singh et al. mentions, '[T]his brotherhood and humanitarian perspective took on a regional and geopolitical tone when China's disinformation campaign targeted India's vaccine diplomacy. Thus, in geopolitical terms, India had a difficult year because of China's aggressive actions along the Line of Actual Control and the COVID-19 pandemic.'[84] Concurrently, we saw articles appearing on different media platforms suggesting that India should buy Chinese vaccines, ignoring the rivalry.[85] It is another matter that the efficacy of the Chinese vaccine became more questionable after the surge in Covid-19 infections on an unprecedented scale in China in December 2022.

US Pharma Lobby and India

The pharma lobby is a very strong lobby in the USA and the West, with deep pockets and enormous political and media clout. This lobby tried hard to sell its vaccines to India and other countries of the Global South. It, in fact, negotiated hard with the GoI to sell its vaccines for India's mammoth domestic vaccine drive. It was not successful because it

---

[84]Singh, Bawa, et al., 'India's Neighbourhood Vaccine Diplomacy During COVID-19 Pandemic: Humanitarian and Geopolitical Perspectives', *Journal of Asian and African Studies,* Volume 58, No. 6, http://tinyurl.com/4ra7wku3. Accessed on 9 January 2024.

[85]Mukherjee, Andy, 'Why India Should Buy Chinese Vaccines', *Bloomberg,* 28 May 2021, http://tinyurl.com/yckr74tp. Accessed on 9 January 2024.

raised the unreasonable demand to indemnify the vaccine producer by the GoI in case of an adverse reaction and because India was able to produce its own vaccines on a massive scale at a much cheaper cost.[86] The lobby was obviously enraged. We can find many articles questioning Indian stand on the issue.[87] The question here is: were the US lobby and Western media working in tandem?

India's West Asia Outreach

India's health diplomacy and its sustained outreach in the Gulf and the West Asian region was also a cause of concern for forces inimical to larger Indian geopolitical and geostrategic interests. Almost the entire Gulf region has a majority Muslim population. Issues like Islamophobia do ring alarm bells in these countries. With the Modi government in New Delhi, this becomes a doubly potent weapon used by adversaries of the government. Additionally, Indians are working in very large numbers in these countries. They repatriate large amounts of foreign exchange, which helps the Indian economy. India imports a substantial part of its energy requirements from the Gulf countries. It also attracts heavy investments from these oil-rich nations. Painting the present government as anti-Muslim even during its fight against Covid-19 was an attempt to undermine India's diplomatic efforts in this critical part of the world. Many of the media articles, rather habitually, mentioned Gujarat and Delhi riots

---

[86]'Indemnity Issue Holds Up J&J, Pfizer and Moderna Jabs', *Times of India*, 7 July 2021, http://tinyurl.com/3yv7hfsf. Accessed on 9 January 2024.

[87]Roy Chowdhury, Debasish, 'Modi Never Bought Enough COVID-19 Vaccines for India. Now the Whole World Is Paying', *Time*, 28 May 2021, http://tinyurl.com/3urrar77. Accessed on 9 January 2024.

in their reports on Covid-19 in India. There was a deliberate attempt by some media houses to find a communal angle in India's fight against the pandemic.

MISSING STORIES OF COURAGE, SACRIFICES OF INDIANS

There were many stories that showed how the country came together to overcome this humongous crisis; how the common people, government agencies, religious organizations and public and private companies came together to help when migrant labourers were walking back to their villages; how people—rich or poor, Hindu or Muslim—provided food and shelter to the walking millions; how no distinction was made on the basis of caste or religion while helping a fellow citizen; how not a single incident of arson and looting was reported even when millions were out on the roads. The resilience, courage, resolve and resourcefulness of India in times of such a calamity doesn't find much mention in the reports of these international media organizations. The narrative they choose to report is largely negative.

A CRISIS OF CREDIBILITY

A very interesting survey was done by an eminent Delhi-based media institution, the Indian Institute of Mass Communication (IIMC), regarding the Western English media and coverage of Covid-19 in India. An online survey was conducted among the media fraternity, including journalists, media educators, students and others. The survey has very interesting findings. About 60 per cent of those surveyed believed that India-related coverage of Covid-19 pandemic in prominent Western English publications was agenda driven. Only 18 per cent respondents found the coverage fully authentic, while 46 per cent said that it was only partially so. Approximately 29 per cent of those surveyed found India-related Covid-19 reporting in these publications partially or fully biased. Majority of the respondents felt that either international politics, internal politics in India or interest of the pharma companies were the reasons for such bias against India. Over two-thirds (69 per cent) of the respondents noted that such coverage impacted India's international image.[88] Many reports published in Western publications were picked up by Indian English and Indian-language media and presented to its audience as some kind of a gospel truth as it had come from 'reputed foreign media.' 'The survey raises a question over the manner the stories carried by a section of the Western media were further carried in a section of the Indian media,' writes Professor Pramod Kumar, who compiled the survey.[89]

Many senior journalists echoed such sentiments. While chairing a discussion at the IIMC on the same topic, senior journalist Alok Mehta, who has led many newsrooms in Indian media houses and has written many books, opined:

---

[88]Kumar, P. (ed.), *Indian Mediapersons Opine: Coverage of Covid-19 Pandemic in India by Western Media*, Indian Institute of Mass Communication, New Delhi, 2022.

[89]Kumar, P., *Coverage of Covid-19 Pandemic in India by Western Media: A Study of the Opinion of Indian Mediapersons*, Indian Institute of Mass Communication, New Delhi, 2021, p. 111.

'The Indian media should be very careful while taking up stories published in the Western media. They want to throw garbage in our country. We should not spread that garbage all over the country by carrying forward their stories. We should discourage the anti- India reporting of the Western media.' The executive editor of CNN News18, Anand Narasimhan, said: 'What happens in my house is my internal matter, I don't want any outsider to lecture me on it.... I do not allow you to fly your drones over my crematoriums unless you allow me to do the same in your country.'[90]

Professor Kumar writes in the abstract of the paper presented on the survey that the Western media started the coverage of the pandemic in India on the premise that, as a developing country, India was ill equipped to deal with the crisis. It did not believe that the country had the knowhow, scientific manpower and research capabilities to develop Covid-19 vaccines. That's why it started doubting the efficacy of domestically developed Covid-19 vaccines as soon as the Indian government announced it.

While one can debate and discuss the IIMC survey, its methodology, sample size, analysis tools, findings, etc., we need to remember that the IIMC is one of the most credible and popular journalism schools in India, which has shaped many renowned media professionals and editors. It has a great faculty, and the school has consistently been ranked as the top mass communication college in India over the years. Its alumni adorn some of the biggest newsrooms in India.

Further, one may argue that the opinions expressed by a few journalists in a survey cannot be taken as a referendum

[90]Ibid.

on Western media's approach on India. This argument is true for any survey undertaken anywhere, on any issue. Surveys provide you only a broad direction. It can be taken only as an indicator of a pattern.

THE GOVERNMENT'S RESPONSE

The lockdown announced by the government was something that was done as a necessity to safeguard the population from the devastation the virus could cause. At that time, this probably was the only available remedy to prevent the virus from spreading rapidly. Most of the public health experts in the world prescribed the non-pharmaceutical interventions (NPIs) as the only available remedy to stop the spread of the infections at that point of time. If you see the Covid-19 timeline in the country, India was preparing its people for the lockdown during early March.

The lockdown in India was indeed very daunting for the daily-wage workers and other poor Indians. But it was the only possible solution suggested by most public health experts to stop Covid-19 from wreaking more havoc. Complete lockdown did take away the livelihood of millions of Indians who had no means to support their families.[91] But did the society at large, the country and the government stop there and did nothing to help its vulnerable citizens as many of the reports cited previously claimed? It must be put on record that the entire nation stood up for its citizens. From

[91]PTI, '2020: The Year Millions of Indians in Informal Sector got Mired in Poverty', *Mint*, 26 December 2020, https://tinyurl.com/8paz8y3x. Accessed on 6 December 2023.

NGOs, political parties, religious organizations, social outfits and local media, to middle-class Indians, upper-middle-class Indians, rural communities, urban citizens, small and big companies and corporates—everyone came together to help those in trouble. The central, state and local governments and their officials worked in cohesion to deliver food, medication and other essentials to those who needed it.[92] Professionals from all walks of life, such as doctors, nurses, ambulance operators, support staff, municipal workers, government officials and law enforcement agencies like police and paramilitary organizations, worked relentlessly to ease the pain caused by the pandemic.

The GoI and its political and administrative leadership created a process-driven mechanism so that essentials were supplied to the citizens who needed them. The most crucial thing at that point of time was to ensure food security to the marginal population, which was indeed accomplished. This information does not find place in most of the international coverage. Some of the steps taken by the government which were prominently reported by the local media[93] are listed here:

1. 800 million people were being given 5 kg of wheat or rice and 1 kg of pulses of their choice free of cost till November 2020. It actually was extended till December 2022.[94]

---

[92]'India Distributed Food Grains to Over 80.74 Crore People During Lockdown. Here's How', *Better India*, 29 July 2020, https://tinyurl.com/3ea7ucm3. Accessed on 6 December 2023.

[93]Saha, Paulomi and Ashok Singhal, '80 करोड़ लोगों को अगले एक साल तक मलिता रहेगा फरी राषन केंद्र सरकार का बड़ा फैसला', *Aaj Tak*, 23 December 2024, http://tinyurl.com/4f2p6jc7. Accessed on 9 January 2024.

[94]Ibid.

2. 200 million female Jan Dhan Bank account holders were given ₹500 per month from April to June 2020.[95]
3. Wages under MGNREGA increased from ₹182 to ₹202 per day, benefitting more than 130 million families.[96]
4. ₹1,000 was given to 30 million senior citizens, widows and disabled people.[97]
5. Under the PM Kisan Yojana, in the first week of April, the government deposited ₹2,000 in each account of more than 80 million farmers.[98]
6. Under the Garib Kalyan Rojgar Abhiyan, an amount of ₹50,000 crore ($663.07 billion) was planned to be spent for the creation of sustainable infrastructure across the country, with the objective to provide livelihood opportunities to the workers.[99]

Many other economic measures were taken to help loan repayment by middle-class Indians and the industry alike. The purpose of enlisting the steps to support the livelihood of the poor is to only demonstrate that the poor were not left at

[95]'Direct Cash Transfer to Women PMJDY Account Holders under PM Garib Kalyan Package for the Month of April 2020 in the Light of COVID-19 Pandemic', *Press Information Bureau*, 3 April 2020, http://tinyurl.com/bdh74ea3. Accessed on 9 January 2024.

[96]'Funds Under Garib Kalyan Rojgar Abhiyaan', *Ministry of Labour & Employment, Government of India*, 24 March 2022, http://tinyurl.com/a3z8hu9f. Accessed on 9 January 2024.

[97]'Pradhan Mantri Garib Kalyan Package', *National Portal of India*, http://tinyurl.com/yckt49ed. Accessed on 9 January 2024.

[98]Ibid.

[99]'Funds Under Garib Kalyan Rojgar Abhiyaan', *Ministry of Labour & Employment, Government of India*, 24 March 2022, http://tinyurl.com/a3z8hu9f. Accessed on 9 January 2024.

the mercy of 'wolves' [100] as one report had claimed.

∽

The art of narrative building is like taking care of an orchard. A narrative needs watering, de-weeding, manuring and pruning from time to time. Narrative building is a continuous work in progress. It needs to be nurtured and kept alive in different stories. A look at some of the headlines and phrases used in the stories listed in the annexure to this book makes them look like they have been taken from political manifestos of parties in India, rather than being an objective assessment of a critical situation like the pandemic. Some of these were insensitive towards India and Indians. Many of them are decidedly anti-Hindu. These come from either politically coloured glasses or an imperialist narrative. While any media outfit is free to criticize the government and its policies, it smacks of bias when it covers only one side of the story. A newspaper can decide as to who it chooses to write its opinion pieces. However, when almost all contributors are known and declared critics of the ruling deposition, the newspaper can't claim to be objective and impartial.

[100]Dhillon, Amrit, 'As the Wealthy Quaff Wine in Comfort, India's Poor Are Thrown to the Wolves', *Guardian*, https://tinyurl.com/296wzdmf. Accessed on 21 November 2023.

Chapter 6

INDIA STILL A LAND OF SNAKE CHARMERS?

During the great Mahabharata War, as the Kauravas were losing to the Pandavas, someone asked Prince Duryodhana if he regretted his actions. A lot of blood had been shed and numerous lives had been lost, including several in the immediate families of both Pandavas and Kauravas. Duryodhana was asked the rationale behind triggering the war when the bloodshed could have been avoided. Did he not know that what he was doing was not in accordance with Dharma? Duryodhana gave a very intriguing answer. He said, 'जानामि धर्मं न च मे प्रवृत्ति–जानामि पापं न च में निवृत्तिः (I knew what I was doing was not in compliance with dharma. However, I was bound by my *pravritti*).'[1] What is this 'pravritti' that Duryodhana was talking about?

'Pravitti' can be roughly translated as the attitude, behaviour or disposition of any human being. It is like the

[1]*Pandav Gita Evam Hans Gita*, Gita Press, Gorakhpur, 2001, p. 34.

innate pattern of habits developed over a period of time and very difficult to change. The Western media is also bound by its habit of patronizing the developing countries, many of them being former colonies. They perpetuate the stereotypical images of India and other countries of the Global South to demean and look down upon.

THE COBRA STORY

While Covid-19 was taking a heavy toll on the world, including India, a local crime story involving a cobra in Kerala was able to find a prominent place in many of the mainstream Western publications.[2] This story is a classic case of the Western media's perception of India and its construction and feeding of a cliched narrative in the minds of the Western population. The story goes like this: a man in Thiruvananthapuram, Kerala, had killed his wife using a poisonous cobra on 6 May 2020. The police had found that the husband had indeed let loose the cobra in his wife's bed. The cobra bit the lady, and she died. The Kerala Police had swung into action and arrested the accused. The husband, after a trial by a local court, was found guilty of murder and has since been jailed. This story is, no doubt, an interesting crime story. The local newspapers carried the story. Other national newspapers and publications treated this as a crime story. The international news agency AFP also spotted it and filed the story. However, this local crime news story was strangely picked up and prominently displayed by many of

---

[2]'Indian Man Arrested For Allegedly Killing Wife with Cobra', *Telegraph*, 25 May 2020, https://tinyurl.com/5ty4vwjt. Accessed on 6 December 2023.

the important Western media publications. The story was published on 25 and 26 May 2020 in the *Telegraph*, *Daily Mail*, *South China Morning Post*, *Mirror*, *Sky News* and *Gulf News* to name a few.[3]

Not only was the story given a prominent place, it was also sensationalized in unusual ways. While a few newspapers used the file pictures of the man and his deceased wife, which presumably were supplied by the news agency, many publications including the *Telegraph*,[4] *Gulf News*[5] and *South China Morning Post*[6] used pictures of cobras in different poses from their picture libraries and displayed them with the story. These pictures of a cobra with its fangs on display, in a sense, had no connection with Kerala's local crime story. The picture captions in the stories filed by these media institutions do not clarify that these pictures are unrelated to the case and were taken from the stock library. The publications should have carried a disclaimer for using a stock photograph so that the readers were not misled. The picture of the cobra with the news sensationalizes the story and possibly makes it more marketable. However, the publication of a local crime story from Kerala in international publications raises a few questions about how India is perceived by editors at Western media houses. The main job of news editors is to decide the priority order of stories competing for limited space in

---

[3]Ibid.

[4]Ibid.

[5]IANS, 'Kerala Woman Killed by Snake: Reptile Exhumed for Forensic Probe', *Gulf News*, 26 May 2020, http://tinyurl.com/bdf4f883. Accessed on 8 January 2024.

[6]Agence France-Presse, 'Indian Man Accused of Using a Cobra to Kill His Wife, after First Trying and Failing with a Viper', *South China Morning Post*, 25 May 2020, https://tinyurl.com/yf8nvpr2. Accessed on 6 December 2023.

a newspaper. When such calls are taken, the mindset of the editors is revealed. Let's examine if there were any competing stories from India during the same time frame.

The day 25 May 2020 was the sixty-second day of the lockdown in India. Covid-19 and the subsequent lockdown in India were being widely covered in these newspapers. The number of cases was increasing rapidly, with 6,977 new cases reported daily. Importantly, this was the highest spike in a day since the reporting of the first case in India in January that, incidentally, was also reported in Kerala.[7] The total number of people who died of Covid-19 had reached 4,021, with 154 deaths on the day itself. The total number of cases had reached 138,845.[8] Though the number of cases was still lower than those in Europe and other Western countries, the ferocious onslaught of the first Covid-19 wave in India had really gathered pace and momentum.

There were at least three Indian stories that were important enough to be considered for space in these foreign publications in the same time frame:

1. Movement of migrant workers[9]
2. Prime Minister Modi chairing a meeting with three services chiefs on India–China tensions in Ladakh[10]

---

[7]Andrews, M.A., et al., 'First Confirmed Case of COVID-19 Infection in India: A Case Report', *Indian Journal of Medical Research*, Vol. 151, No. 5, 2020, http://tinyurl.com/ynn4u78w. Accessed on 8 January 2024.

[8]'Coronavirus News May 25 Highlights: Total Cases at Almost 1,40,000; Maharashtra Spikes by 2,400', *CNBC TV 18*, 26 May 2020, http://tinyurl.com/bdesfavf. Accessed on 8 January 2024.

[9]PTI, '4 Crore Migrant Workers in India; 75 Lakh Return Home So Far: MHA', *Times of India*, 24 May 2020, http://tinyurl.com/yvf3d8xk. Accessed on 8 January 2024.

[10]Roche, Elizabeth, 'PM Modi Holds Consultations with 3 Service Chiefs and

3. Indian Council of Medical Research's (ICMR's) go-ahead for testing hydroxychloroquine for the treatment of Covid-19[11]

MIGRANT WORKERS RETURNING

The movement of migrant workers from different Indian states was a big news item that had attracted media attention worldwide. Earlier, the stories on migrant workers' movement had been covered very prominently in the above-cited publications. The Indian Railways had announced that it had carried 35 lakh migrant workers to their homes from different cities in the country. The announcement had been made at a press conference by the home ministry. Officials had said that in total, 75 lakh workers were ferried: 40 lakhs by buses and 35 lakhs by Shramik Special trains. A total of 2,600 trains had been deployed between 1 May 2020 and 23 May 2020 when the announcement was made.[12] It was a significant occasion and an achievement by all standards. Since the publications had earlier carried stories on migrant workers, this development was surely relevant and newsworthy to them. Majority of the stories on domestic migration filed by these publications had been extremely critical of the government. Therefore, a sense of fairness demanded that the

---

NSA amid China Tensions along the LAC', *Mint*, 26 May 2020, http://tinyurl.com/y456vj3a. Accessed on 8 January 2024.

[11]PTI, 'No Major Side-Effects of HCQ in Studies in India, Can Be Used as Preventive Covid Treatment: ICMR', *Hindustan Times*, 26 May 2020, http://tinyurl.com/5bw5n2r6. Accessed on 8 January 2024.

[12]PTI, '4 Crore Migrant Workers in India; 75 Lakh Return Home So Far: MHA', *Tribune*, 23 May 2022, http://tinyurl.com/34vdyhpc. Accessed on 8 January 2024.

announcement by the Indian home ministry be considered for publication by these media outfits. However, it was ignored.

INDIA–CHINA TENSION IN LADAKH

An important story from the international news perspective was concurrently developing in India. It had to do with India–China border tensions on the Ladakh front. Hectic troop movement from both countries had taken place, with Chinese troops trying to ingress the Indian side of the Line of Actual Control (LAC).[13] About 25 days later, on 15 June, the tension resulted in a bloody clash at Galwan Valley in Ladakh, where 20 Indian soldiers were martyred.[14] It was the bloodiest skirmish between the two armies in the last 45 years. The number of Chinese soldiers killed during the clash was reported to be much higher than officially accepted by China. The TASS reported that 45 Chinese soldiers had died in the clash.[15] Prime Minister Modi had chaired a crucial meeting with three chiefs of defence forces on the issue, indicating increase in military activities.[16] The PM meeting the top army

[13]The LAC refers to the line of control on the eastern border of India with China. The actual border is not clearly demarcated with both countries having counterclaims.

[14]'Text of Raksha Mantri Shri Rajnath Singh Statement in Rajya Sabha on September 17', *Press Information Bureau*, 17 September 2020, http://tinyurl.com/5c45uuv2. Accessed on 8 January 2024.

[15]Dutta, P., '45 Chinese Soldiers Died in Galwan, Reports Russian News Agency TASS', *India Today*, 11 February 2021, http://tinyurl.com/yn69zsk7. Accessed on 8 January 2024.

[16]India News, 'PM Meets NSA, Chief of Defence Staff over India-China Face-Off in Ladakh', *NDTV*, http://tinyurl.com/8knxfwkv. Accessed on 8 January 2024.

commanders in the context of escalating border tension with China was surely a story to be considered. This was a very important development from a geopolitical perspective. In any case, the China–India flare up was a developing international story that deserved attention from these publications.

HYDROXYCHLOROQUINE

Another development related to the treatment of Covid-19 was reported by the Indian media during these two days. The medicine hydroxychloroquine was given permission by the ICMR and WHO to be used as treatment for Covid-19. Remember, these were the days when any possible drug for Covid-19 management was of huge news value. Hydroxychloroquine is a drug that is generally used for the prevention and treatment of malaria. India had banned the export of the drug, as it was being touted to be effective in curbing infections and there was a domestic need for it. Hydroxychloroquine was a firm presence in international news, as then US President Donald Trump had threatened India a month earlier in April 2020 to lift the ban or face consequences.[17] It surely was newsworthy for consideration by these publications.

COBRA TRUMPS ALL

All these three stories were covered by Indian news agencies and media in some detail. However, none of these stories

---

[17]'Hydroxychloroquine: The Unproven "Corona Drug" Trump Is Threatening India for', *BBC News*, 7 April 2020, http://tinyurl.com/4kyd8n4z. Accessed on 8 January 2024.

found a prominent place in the aforementioned international publications. Instead, the cobra story was covered in great detail with stock images.

It is the sole discretion of the editor as to what they consider important for their readers. What goes in a newspaper or on a news website is the sole prerogative of its editor. Several arguments may be given for or against the inclusion or exclusion of a particular story, and all these arguments are valid one way or the other. However, it is also true that the choice of including or excluding a particular story or news event surely reveals the bias of the editor and the publication.

The whole purpose of mentioning this episode is to demonstrate how influential Western media houses have deep-rooted biases when they look at India. The cobra story received prominence in Western publications because it furthered the stereotypical narrative about India. Western societies have been fed with an imagery of India by its media and opinion-makers through ages. India is considered as the land of snake charmers. The cobra story, thus, becomes a natural feed to fortify such a clichéd narrative.

A person sitting in the newsroom doesn't even think twice before selecting such a story over others for its readers. It goes perfectly with the editorial line and perception of India within the media. In fact, it sometimes looks so routine to carry such an item that any argument against it may be considered flimsy. Someone may say, 'What is a big deal if the cobra story was carried in the publications?' Some in the Western newsrooms may consider it very normal as it is an interesting crime story. But it needs to be understood by the media fraternity in the West that it is not acceptable to stereotype a country like this. Such narrative is decidedly negative and detrimental to the interests of the country and its people. It hurts the pride of almost all Indians living in India and abroad. The prominent coverage given to the cobra crime story while neglecting other developments during the first wave of Covid-19 can surely be considered a part of conscious negative-image building of India by the Western media.

While the Western media houses may not have a large presence in India in terms of circulation and subscription numbers, they have a disproportionately huge impact in terms of their ability to shape larger narratives and opinions. They are read by influencers and policy-makers, and their reports are reproduced in many Indian-language publications. These also often become points of reference, and, thus, help set the agenda. A few international English media publications have an unjustifiable amount of clout in Indian polity. Surprisingly, most of them have only a couple of correspondents posted in India and a very sparse local or grassroots reporting mechanism.

India is a vast country with multi-layered political, economic, linguistic and social structures. But those representing most of the dominant Western English media outfits form opinions based on interactions and conversations with a handful of opinionated English-speaking local journalists, intellectuals or experts in large cities like Delhi or Mumbai. These opinions are then presented as facts and gospel truths.

THE NEW YORK TIMES RECRUITMENT ADVERTISEMENT AND FREEDOM OF EXPRESSION

The *New York Times* published a recruitment advertisement in early July 2021.[18] The advertisement was for a New Delhi-based position heading the business and economic coverage. The position also included coverage of the entire South Asian region, including Pakistan, Bangladesh, Nepal, Sri Lanka, Bhutan and Maldives. In a sense, the person was to lead the South Asia Business and Economic Bureau of the *New York Times*. The advertisement was published at a time when the deadly second wave of the pandemic was sweeping India.

In its detailed description of the position, the advertisement read:

> India's future now stands at a crossroads. Mr. Modi is advocating a self-sufficient, muscular nationalism centred on the country's Hindu majority. That vision puts him at odds with the interfaith, multicultural goals of modern India's founders. The government's growing efforts to police online speech and media discourse have raised difficult questions about balancing issues of security and privacy with free speech. Technology is both a help and a hindrance.[19]

The advertisement generated a fierce debate in Indian media when it was published. It also created an uproar on social media across the country. It is important to

---

[18]@kanchangupta, *X* (formerly Twitter), 2 July 2021, 1.09 p.m., http://tinyurl.com/4jy4ekkk. Accessed on 11 January 2024. The advertisement was later deleted on the New York Times's website.

[19]Ibid.

analyse the *New York Times* advertisement, as it explains a mindset issue that prevails in an important Western media publication. [20]

The section of the advertisement quoted previously reads more like an opinion piece than a statement of facts. The sentiments expressed in the advertisement elicited a justifiable outcry among Indian citizens. Several commentators criticized the advertisement as being 'biased', 'anti-Modi' and 'anti-Hindu'. Many found it rather unusual for a publication to recruit a person on the basis of a particular political viewpoint. It also seemed to deviate from the norm because a similar kind of advertisement during the same period for a posting in Hong Kong had no such mention. A commentary on the Indian news website *Newslaundry* stated:

> It is also at odds with NYT's usual postings for jobs. For example, a current opening for a staff editor in Hong Kong includes no context about tensions with China, the national security law, or the pro-democracy protests that have dominated the region over the past two years. This opening for an investigative correspondent in Asia, who would be based out of Seoul, is also without any mention about political scenarios of the region.[21]

It is clear that on the pretext of giving context, the newspaper decided to take an ideological stance in the domestic politics of India. It indicated that it will recruit a person who will head the India bureau only if they have a particular

---

[20]Sodhi, Tanishka, 'Did NYT's Job Posting for a Business Correspondent in India Deserve the Outrage It Got?', *Newslaundry*, 8 July 2021, http://tinyurl.com/53wywbux. Accessed on 12 January 2024.

[21]Ibid.

political view of the Indian government. It also seemed to articulate that the person had to be anti-Modi. It wilfully tried to divide the country along communal and religious lines by using politically loaded phrases like 'muscular nationalism' and 'Hindu majority'. The advertisement, thus, showed its communal and ideological biases. The spirit of the advertisement was against the established norms of neutrality but also against the core guiding values of the New York Times, which it is very proud of.

The opening page of the company's website gives details of its mission and values. It says:

> We seek the truth and help people understand the world. This mission is rooted in our belief that great journalism has the power to make each reader's life richer and more fulfilling, and all of society stronger and more just. Over a hundred years ago, The Times pledged 'to give the news impartially, without fear or favour, regardless of party, sect, or interests involved.' That commitment remains true today: We follow the truth, wherever it leads.[22]

As is clear among other ideals, the newspaper company talks about seeking the truth, impartiality and journalism without fear or favour, regardless of party, sect or interests involved. Its mission also talks of a just society. But in the opinion expressed in its advertisement for a senior editorial position in India, was the company true to its stated ideals?

It may be noted that we are not talking of a news item, an editorial or even an opinion piece published in the

[22]http://tinyurl.com/2c7rfaeu. Accessed on 12 January 2024.

newspaper. A newspaper and its editors, correspondents and other writers are entitled to have an opinion and express it without fear. But in this case, it was an advertisement to recruit a senior editorial professional who will not only cover India but the entire South Asia for many years. By prescribing a political viewpoint in its recruitment advertisement, was the New York Times not asking that only people having a particular political and ideological opinion should apply? Or worse, that if you had any different opinion than stated in the advertisement, you had no place in its India bureau. It amounted to discrimination on the basis of political opinion, which is essentially anti-democratic.

India, like the USA, is a democratic society where freedom of expression is the backbone of the system. The entire edifice of a democracy rests on it. Freedom of expression is fundamental to any democratic structure, more so in the Indian context, as India is a civilizational democracy. This declared political untouchability and discrimination by the newspaper on the basis of political views, thus, was not only against the principles of equality but against the constitutional tenets of justice and fundamental rights as well.

Judging by the standards that the newspaper has outlined for itself, it is clear that the said advertisement did not subscribe to the company values. The *New York Times*'s opinionated editors may not like it but PM Narendra Modi is a democratically elected PM as per the Indian Constitution. The Indian elections are conducted by the Election Commission of India, a statutory and independent body. The Indian electoral process is considered impartial and credible the world over. While the newspaper has all the right to question the policies of the Modi government, it surely failed in its professed journalistic obligation of 'impartiality'. It tried to establish the political opinion of its editors as fact and truth. It demonized Hindus and communalized the recruitment process of a key posting in India.

In demonizing Hindus, did it not castigate the entire faith? Is it a crime that India is a 'Hindu-majority' nation? The present editors of the newspaper may have opinions against the policies and style of politics of the ruling party in India, but by mandating that its future staffers have to follow their opinions, were they not suppressing plurality, openness and freedom of choice within the institution? By doing so, it tried to meddle in the domestic politics of India. It was far from the high ideals of truth, impartiality, fairness and justice as claimed by the newspaper in its own mission statement.

∽

The Cobra story, the Mangalyaan cartoon published by the *New York Times* in September 2014 and the recruitment advertisement in the paper show that the prominent Western news publications have a penchant for showing India in a negative light. Whenever this is analysed and serious questions are raised on such coverages, it is often defended as the 'freedom of expression' of the journalist or the 'press freedom' as enshrined in the Constitution of India. However, it is a flawed logic as is proved by the recruitment advertisement. The tone and language used in the advertisement proves beyond any doubt that the anti-India stories published by the paper indeed come from the editorial line as decided by its management. It is not the case of media freedom. The anti-India bias of the paper has turned into anti-Modi bias after 2014.

Chapter 7

COLONIZATION OF MINDS

'And they dress up like white men,
As if they are in the white man's country...'[1]

The above lines from the poem 'Song of Lawino' by the famous Ugandan poet Okot p'Bitek sum up the conflicts that almost all developing societies face. The poem underlines the pain of Lawino, an African woman whose husband Ocol had become completely Westernized and brought home a woman with Western habits, and started neglecting his wife. The poem describes how he had cut himself off completely from his roots, culture, traditions and environment. The poem brings to the fore his total alienation from his civilizational values. The lament of Lawino poignantly speaks of the deep emotional scars and cultural conflicts inflicted by the Western narrative on societies and

[1]p'Bitek, Okot, 'Song of Lawino', *Song of Lawino: And Song of Ocol,* East African Educational Publisher Limited, House, Nairobi, 1966, p. 48.

peoples of Asia, Africa and Latin America. One may argue that things have changed since the poem was written in the 1960s. But has the ground reality really changed? Have we—the formerly colonized—been able to actually free ourselves from the shackles of the white man's shadow?

THE WESTERN NARRATIVE CONTINUES

One ideal example of Western narrative is how Indian vaccines were initially treated by the British establishment in September 2021. Indians fully vaccinated with Oxford AstraZeneca vaccines were considered unvaccinated and were made to undergo 10 days of forced quarantine.[2] It led to an outrage in India. Another instance would be the war in Ukraine, where two European nations are fighting. The West's media outfits are depicting this story as a precursor to the third World War and cajoling countries such as India to take sides.[3] A war in Europe is much more important for the Western media than anywhere else. Poorer countries of Asia, such as Iraq, Afghanistan and Sri Lanka, are too easily forgotten after misguided adventures, be it by the so-called 'free world' or the erstwhile USSR's communist regimes. To illustrate, the situation in Afghanistan where both the USA and erstwhile USSR competed for control was relegated to margins after the war in Ukraine. Anything happening

---

[2]'Covid: UK Faces Rising Backlash over Selective Vaccine Policy', *Times of India*, 23 September 2021, https://tinyurl.com/w5bn9afm. Accessed on 4 December 2023.

[3]Borger, Julian, 'Russia's Invasion of Ukraine Crystallises Divide between US Allies and Rest', *Guardian*, 26 March 2022, https://tinyurl.com/ya5vshd2. Accessed on 7 December 2023.

in their neighbourhood is a world issue, whereas bigger calamities elsewhere are described as local happenings. Right now, the Western media is more concerned with the power games played between Russia and NATO over Ukraine, while sermonizing countries like India as to what it should do.[4] India's External Affairs Minister Dr S. Jaishankar bluntly enunciated, 'Europe has to grow out of the mindset that Europe's problems are the world's problems, but the world's problems are not Europe's problems.'[5] He was referring to the Russia–Ukraine conflict and the Western media's constant suggestions for India to take an anti-Russia stand. The Western powers were irritated with the stand taken by India. The Western media carried out this narrative. This narrative building on behalf of the West is continued by the Western media.

When it comes to real-world issues, the West and its media seem to pay lip service only. Even though the Western media is more nuanced now, the old colonial narrative continues nonetheless. It uses politically correct phrases and arguments that are in vogue. The biases and discriminations are more sophisticated now. There was discrimination even during tragedies such as Covid-19. The wealthy nations of the West hoarded Covid-19 vaccines when some countries in Africa had not even been able to vaccinate 1 per cent of their people with the first dose. A few wealthy nations had

[4]Mogul, Rhea, 'India's Words Are Anti-War, but New Delhi's Actions Are Propping Up Putin's Regime', *CNN*, 4 October 2022, https://tinyurl.com/242xpnsz. Accessed on 7 December 2023.

[5]Barman, S., 'Europe Has to Grow Out of Mindset That Its Problems Are World's Problems: Jaishankar', *Indian Express*, 4 June 2022, http://tinyurl.com/3ur5ncdc. Accessed on 19 January 2024.

stockpiles of vaccines which was more than the requirements of their entire populations. Many in European countries and the USA had started taking booster doses at a time when many in other countries had not got the first dose.[6]

When the market economy expanded, the media further became an important part of the international economic and financial structures. Colonization, imperial conquests and subsequent loot of the rest of the world by the West were precursors to the present-day complex world financial systems. As seen previously, the Western media was a creation of imperialism and the market economy and, till date, depends on that very system for its survival and sustenance.

The media is market driven and dependent on advertising revenue, which mainly comes from industries and government sources. Its claims of being an independent watchdog are phoney and hollow at a conceptual level. If the Western media is a product of the capitalist system, how can it claim that it is independent of the system? It is subservient to the world order created by the West, with the Anglo-Saxon civilization at the centre of the universe. The rest of the world is only seen and covered in the media with that prism. The Western media builds and sustains that narrative as an important tool of this assumed civilizational supremacy.

A Sociocultural Context

The information business also has a civilizational and cultural context. The idea of civilization against 'barbarism' was

---

[6]Psaledakis, D., 'Developing Nation's Plea to World's Wealthy at U.N.: Stop Vaccine Hoarding', *Reuters*, 23 September 2021, http://tinyurl.com/ybvt5bvu. Accessed on 19 January 2024.

developed by eighteenth-century French thinkers, claims Samuel P. Huntington in his celebrated book *The Clash of Civilisations and The Remaking of World Order*. He stipulates that a civilized society is 'settled, urban and literate'[7] against a primitive society. This 'fundamental' premise is very Western and flawed. So, if one is not in an urban setting and is not literate as per Western standards, one is considered to be a part of a primitive society. Therefore, the imperial powers thought they were doing a great service to the conquered societies by transforming them from primitive to modern by 'civilizing' them. The Indian civilization, for example, that has survived over millennia, was considered 'primitive' as per this thinking because it was predominantly rural.

SAREE NOT MODERN ENOUGH FOR DINNER

An upmarket restaurant in New Delhi's posh locality did not allow a diner to enter, as she was wearing a saree. While denying the entry, the staff supposedly told the diner that 'we only allow smart casuals. And saree doesn't come under smart casuals.'[8] The incident happened in September 2021 and obviously created quite a stir in the media. People protested this discrimination against the saree-wearing woman and the restaurant had to apologize. The incident may look trivial on the face of it. However, it raises some basic and fundamental questions for society.

---

[7]Huntington, Samuel P., *The Clash of Civilizations and the Remaking of World Order*, Simon & Schuster, 2011, p. 40.

[8]Kalra, Sanchita, 'Furore over Delhi Restaurant Not Allowing Saree', *Hindustan Times*, 29 September 2021, http://tinyurl.com/23c4d3h8. Accessed on 8 January 2024.

The saree incident is not an isolated one. Many such instances occur routinely in India when people are segregated and divided on the basis of sense of dressing, eating habits, looks and the language they speak. Such incidents can be observed in many other developing societies as well.

Lawino, in the poem mentioned above, is described as 'regressive' because she wears ethnic African dresses and ornaments. The poem and the incident both demonstrate a scornful attitude towards one's own culture and dress. It is sad that such an attitude has been internalized to an extent that it does not raise any alarm in the common man's mind. Such incidents are treated as minor events by the media to get more eyeballs or make a news item viral. However, nothing is done beyond lip service.

Even though India and Uganda are separated by thousands of miles and a huge gap in the time period, what the fictitious character Lawino felt in a poem penned in the previous century in Uganda resonates with what the diner experienced in India in 2021. Such scorn towards one's own culture reflects imperialism of a new order. It speaks of how deep the colonial roots have penetrated. Centuries of constant conditioning have changed habits, behaviours and notions of what is desirable and what is not. Emulation of erstwhile colonial masters is considered modern and fashionable.

A NEW FORM OF IMPERIALISM

The previous two centuries have witnessed a vast expansion of communication systems and mass media, which indeed has brought the world closer and opened new vistas of cooperation for the development of societies. The West has almost total control over collection, storage and dissemination of information. It has resulted in a new kind of mental subjugation of the developing world by the developed world. While the spurt of nationalist movements across Asia, Africa and Latin America during the last century dismantled colonialism, the mental subjugation of these societies continues. A new form of imperialism is the colonization of minds. The irony is that India, which has thousands of years of value systems, is forced to look at itself from the borrowed and often imposed Western lens.

As part of the previous processes of colonization, the imperial powers physically controlled the landmass and the instruments of state of Third-World countries. However, the colonization of minds or cultural imperialism is the process by which powerful cultural and political Western systems exert influence and control over thoughts, beliefs, values, perceptions, preferences, habits, choices and behaviours of individuals and communities in the developing world. It occurs through various means, including education, news, cinema, television, literature, language, religion and socialization.

In the context of historical colonialism, colonization of minds was always an integral part of the colonial project. The colonizers imposed their own cultural, social, intellectual and, very often, religious frameworks onto the colonized population. This was done by suppressing, wilfully degrading or erasing indigenous knowledge; demeaning local traditions; converting faiths; languages; and imposing the colonizer's values, beliefs, institutional frameworks, religious practices, political structures and systems of administration and governance. The Indian statesman and diplomat K.M. Panikkar writes that 'political domination brought in its train a doctrine of racialism and a feeling of European solidarity as against the Asians.' He adds that Europe, with its social, economic and political structures and industrial power, 'challenged the basis of Asian societies; it imposed its will on them and brought about social and political changes in Asia which are of fundamental importance.'[9] He also writes that there was an urge to Christianize Asia among the European imperialist powers. Each of the imperial powers competed with each other to convert more and more natives to the imported faith—Christianity. He says that the Asian societies' religious, philosophical systems, mental outlooks and material set-ups have undergone changes which are beyond estimation.[10]

This new form of colonization further involves the manipulation of information, fake news, misinformation campaigns, narratives and ideologies to control and dominate the way people perceive and understand the world around them. The West has invested in state and non-state institutions that complement each other and perpetuate this modern-day slavery of minds.

When the Cold War started, both capitalist and communist Western systems competed to control cultural space and media in the erstwhile colonies and other newly emerged states. These developing countries became battle grounds for both these ideologies. It created divisions and left deep scars among native people.

The alien, Western concepts have been so deeply

---

[9]Panikkar, K.M., *Asia and Western Dominance*, George Allan and Unwin Ltd., London, 1953, pp. 14–18.

[10]Ibid. 479.

internalized in these societies that even when some sections try to break away from them, they are declared as regressive. In a way, a deep division has been created within the Third-World societies, where a small but powerful elite becomes an advocate of imposed Western narratives. This elite, which has been educated in the institutions run on Western principles and has curriculum devised along similar lines, converses in the language that the 'masters' spoke and has become vociferous proponents of the so-called universal and modern culture. This modernization is more of Westernization. Inherent in this discourse is the negation of anything native.

The Third-World societies are mostly treated as footnotes by the Western media so far as its daily news coverages are concerned. Western cultural extravaganza, awards, entertainment shows, celebrities, sports, festivals, events, cinema and political happenings are presented as universal, international and world events. The West's control on these soft power instruments is almost complete. In fact, more than the political and military power, the West rules the world's mind space with its soft-power machinations. Thus, the independence of Suriname may not be covered even by its Latin American neighbours, but the coronation of a 74-year-old King Charles III of Britain is televised the world over.

DIGITAL MEDIA CONGLOMERATES

The use of the Internet and easy access to digital assets via smartphones have increased our reach to millions almost instantly.

International digital media conglomerates, such as Google, Facebook, Amazon, Microsoft and X, among others, have grown exponentially, amassing vast influence and control over the dissemination of information worldwide. Expansion of global media conglomerates has made their reach far and wide. The use of AI tools has automated not only the delivery mechanisms but also narrative building. Algorithms have become very powerful tools in the hands of a few social and digital media companies. They have created huge and almost uncontrollable monopolies. The colonization of minds through the influence of international digital media conglomerates has become an increasingly significant phenomenon in the modern era. These conglomerates shape and manipulate content to suit their interests. The concentration of power[11] has led to a situation when even sovereignty of nations gets challenged by their executives.[12]

The masters of the Silicon Valley play a crucial role in determining priorities and, thereby, affect the choices that an individual consumer makes. More often than not, they decide the priorities of the content of people's inboxes. They decide as to which stories should receive attention and coverage, effectively shaping public discourse and agenda-setting on a global scale.[13]

---

[11]McEvoy, Jemima, 'GOP Calls Social Media Censorship of Hunter Biden Story "Attempt To Rig An Election"', *Forbes*, 15 October 2020, http://tinyurl.com/pd4curuu. Accessed on 8 January 2024.

[12]Dey, Deepjyoti, 'Social Media and The State Sovereignty: Ethics Vs Encryption', *LinkedIn*, 29 May 2021, http://tinyurl.com/2xnrjmxp. Accessed on 8 January 2024.

[13]Gopalakrishnan, Amulya, 'This Documentary Should Make You Quit Social Media', *Times of India*, 14 September, 2020, https://tinyurl.com/mryj6yx7. Accessed on 6 December 2023.

The local media in developing societies like India almost instinctively follow hashtags or trends on social media, which are open to manipulations by state and non-state actors alike. It can be argued that the social media platforms have helped the creation of digital communities and linked people virtually, thus adding immense value to users. This is only partially true. They have led to the creation of filter bubbles and echo chambers as well. Algorithms employed by these conglomerates often reinforce users' existing beliefs and preferences, limiting exposure to diverse perspectives and contributing to the polarization of societies.[14]

The vast reach and influence of these conglomerates allow them to impact political landscapes, either through targeted advertising or control over user data. They impact the choices individuals make. They have the capacity to influence even the political choices of the citizens, thus raising concerns that they can influence the workings of democratic processes. Local politics is a tough game where different groups and parties jostle for the interests of these conglomerates because tech giants now have capabilities where they can impact the political behaviour of people. They can manufacture issue-based virtual bubbles using algorithms and bots to create social upheaval and political turmoil. There are numerous instances where the host countries have complained that social media organizations play a partisan role in the domestic political situations.

The violence seen on 2021 Republic Day in New Delhi is one example of such a case. A symbol of India's sovereignty and state power, the Red Fort was raided by miscreants on

---

[14]Ibid.

26 January 2021, while Capitol Hill, the symbol of the USA in Washington, D.C., was raided by miscreants on 6 January 2021. The GoI accused social media companies of adopting double standards in dealing with the situation at Red Fort in New Delhi and at Capitol Hill in Washington, D.C., in the USA. The Indian government said that the social media companies had blocked some content showing disturbances at the Capitol Hill while they allowed the Red Fort events with objectionable hashtags, despite legal orders to stop such publication.

In a press release issued after a meeting with X officials, the government objected to the 'differential treatment' to the two incidents.[15] The press note said that it was not 'journalistic freedom' or 'freedom of expression' as per the Indian law but acts of provoking disturbance to the public order. The response of the tech companies to the content published was not in the same vein. India's electronics and information technology minister, Ravi Shankar Prasad, said that 'there should not be double standards. If an attack is there at Capitol Hill (US Congress), then social media supports police action. But if there is an aggressive attack at the Red Fort, the symbol of India's freedom where the prime minister hoists the national flag, you have double standards. This is plainly unacceptable.'[16]

---

[15]'MeitY Issues Press Statement about Meeting of Secretary IT with Twitter Inc. Team', *Press Information Bureau, Government of India*, 10 February 2021, http://tinyurl.com/3x2y5bas. Accessed on 11 January 2024.

[16]'"Double Standards": Govt Reminds Social Media Platforms How They Failed to Act in Red Fort Violence Case', *TimesNowNews*.com, 25 February 2021, http://tinyurl.com/2p9sapkn. Accessed on 8 January 2024.

NEED FOR A NEW WORLD INFORMATION ORDER

The need for a NWIO was never so great as it is today. The world needs new norms to process the flow of information.

As different countries started national news agencies during the second half of the last century, everyone realized that information was key not only during war times, but also during peacetime. Effective communication with and among people was very important for the developing countries. Their efforts towards growth and development hinged greatly on appropriate information flow. While there were many discussions around the subject, serious efforts towards establishing a structural mechanism for better information flow started only in late 1970s and early 1980s.

As a culmination of the ongoing efforts, UNESCO organized a round table conference on the new world information and communication order (NWICO) in September 1983 in Igls, Austria. Its final report states:

> More than 80 percent of all written news was disseminated by four transnational agencies and the average per capita gap between developing and industrialized countries was 1:10.7 for newspaper printing, 1:8.45 for radio sets and 1:15.4 for television sets. The developed countries exported four times as many radios, nine times as many books, 19 times as many television and cassettes and 49 times as much photographic equipment then did the developing countries.[17]

---

[17]Director-General, *Study of Communication Problems—Implementation of Resolutions 4/19 and 4/20. Adopted by the General Conference at Its Twenty-*

The report noted that the discussions on the future of communication was 'too often clouded or distorted by suspicion, misunderstanding, political one-upmanship, cultural ethnocentricity and the desire to dominate, in both the political and economic arenas.'[18] It further said that the world communication systems, thus, appeared to be out of balance.

S. Viswam, a senior Indian journalist and writer, states, 'Three quarters of the world population living in the third world countries are dominated by the Western countries in regard to the global flow of communication. Since the flow is one way, unbalanced and compulsory, the dominance by the Western media of the developing countries turns out veritably to be a modern and sophisticated form of cultural imperialism.'[19]

India's experience in the expansion of affordable Internet services post 2016, when Jio was launched in India, can be emulated in many countries of the Global South to end the West's hegemony over the information industry. With affordable devices now available to individuals in the developing world to access the Internet, information flow within the developing societies will increase. As more people are empowered with information, the Western ecosystem of one-way narrative building will increasingly come under stress. It is high time that credible leadership is built in the Global South to create an alternate information order.

First Session, UNESCO, Paris, 1983, p. 9.

[18]Ibid. 8.

[19]Goyal, D.R. (ed.), *Non-Alignment: Concept and Concerns,* Ajanta Publications, New Delhi, 1986, pp. 241–2.

NEW WORLD INFORMATION ORDER AND INDIA

India and China are likely candidates to carry on this task of creating and nurturing the alternate new order. Both have been the victims of Western narratives and have large economies, trained human manpower, technological prowess and financial resources to take the lead in the area. However, China lacks one of the key ingredients of the Internet-driven information flow driving the world today. The NWIO has to have a grounds-up approach. The government can be a facilitator, but it cannot be a harbinger of the information flow. Content generation, storage, dissemination and access need to stay democratized and in the hands of people. This is the fundamental nature of the new technological advances. While it cannot be left to a few for-profit giants to control the flow, it can also not be completely left in the hands of the government to control it.

China, with its totalitarian regime, Communist Party-controlled Internet and application ecosystem, and desire to control and regulate every bit of its citizens' lives, is ill-suited to lead this initiative. Its conduct during Covid-19, when it chose to conceal relevant information, does not build confidence in the long term. The NWICO can only emerge from a transparent society and system. It cannot hide behind a great wall of secrecy and surveillance. The alternate narrative building will be a long-drawn affair and not a one-time effort. It requires trust, transparency, openness and tolerance for others views and perseverance. The West has perfected this art over centuries. Thus, the alternative will also require humongous efforts, resources and nurturing.

India, with its democracy, free society, deep institutional

framework, civilizational legacy of diversity, plurality, vibrant academia, free media, independent judiciary, private entrepreneurial spirit and knowledge economy, is best suited to build on and lead the quest for the new information and communication order.

Sensing India's potential, the Western media has sharpened its attacks on the country's present leadership. It has created a story that the present setup is intolerant and democratic institutions are in danger. There are indeed faults in India. However, Indian society is open and tenacious enough to overcome these. However, the Western media presents these faults as permanent divisions. Its ongoing offensive against India needs to be seen and analysed from the perspective of offence being the best defence. We have seen how the Western media tried to create a fake narrative during the trying times of Covid-19 by saying that India will not be able to cope up with the challenge. This is against the backdrop of India asserting its civilizational values and challenging the false Western narratives.

The open, diverse and tolerant Indian society can lead the NWICO effort that has to be largely people-driven and cannot be left to the government alone. It is perhaps best for India to lead this battle of narratives as the natural leader of the free Global South. This is a battle to capture the hearts and minds of people. The West has played this game for too long when it appropriated the role of judge, jury, complainant, plaintiff and executioner. India—its government, entrepreneurs, people, media institutions, academia, social sector, political and social leadership—cannot escape its historical responsibility to lead from the front.

ANNEXURE

ARTICLES WITH BIASED CONTENT AGAINST INDIA

S. No.	Date	Publisher	Heading
1	30 March 2020	The Guardian	'As the Wealthy Quaff Wine in Comfort, India's Poor Are Thrown to the Wolves'
2	30 March 2020	The Guardian	'Divided Delhi under Lockdown: "If Coronavirus Doesn't Kill Me, Hunger Will"'
3	31 March 2020	Time	'Modi's Hasty Coronavirus Lockdown of India Leaves Many Fearful for What Comes Next'
4	3 April 2020	Time	'It Was Already Dangerous to Be Muslim in India. Then Came the Coronavirus'
5	6 May 2020	The New York Times	'As India Reopens, Deaths Jump Sharply'
6	12 May 2020	BBC News	'India Coronavirus: Pregnant Student Safoora Zargar at Risk in Jail'
7	12 May 2020	The Independent	'Coronavirus: India's Carbon Emissions Fall for First Time in Four Decades Giving "Window" into Life after Coal'

8	16 May 2020	The New York Times	'Modi's Popularity Soars as India Weathers the Pandemic'
9	17 May 2020	The Wall Street Journal	'India's Coronavirus Crisis Spurs a New Look at Self-Reliance'
10	19 May 2020	The Guardian	'"My Angel": Man Who Became Face of India's Stranded Helped Home by Stranger'
11	25 May 2020	The Telegraph	'India Faces Rural Epidemic as Millions Return to Villages as Curfew Is Eased'
12	27 May 2020	The New York Times	'How Modi Failed the Pandemic Test'
13	30 May 2020	The New York Times	'The Rich Love India's Lockdown. For the Poor It's Another Story'
14	31 May 2020	BBC News	'India Coronavirus: Why Is India Reopening amid a Spike in Cases?'
15	11 June 2020	The Guardian	'Global Report: India Reports Surge in Covid-19 Cases as Lockdown Eased'
16	15 June 2020	BBC News	'Five Key Questions about India's Rising Covid-19 Infections'
17	28 June 2020	BBC News	'Coronavirus: How Delhi "Wasted" Lockdown to Become India's Biggest Hotspot'
18	30 June 2020	BBC News	'Coronavirus: Secrecy Surrounds India PM Narendra Modi's "$1Bn" Covid-19 Fund'
19	17 July 2020	The Telegraph	'Overcrowded Prisons in Kashmir Are "Incubators" for Covid-19 as Inmates Are Refused Release'
20	19 July 2020	The New York Times	'India Rounds Up Critics under Shadow of Virus Crisis, Activists Say'
21	29 July 2020	The Guardian	'Modi's Covid-19 Policies Make Clear that in India Some Lives Matter More Than Others'

22	3 August 2020	The Guardian	'"We Have Abandoned the Poor": Slums Suffer as Covid-19 Exposes India's Social Divide'
23	5 August 2020	The Washington Post	'India Marks Another Day of Erasure and Insult against Its Muslim Citizens'
24	5 August 2020	The Washington Post	'In Modi's Quest to Transform India, a Grand Hindu Temple Rises'
25	6 August 2020	BBC News	'Coronavirus: India Becomes Third Country to Pass Two Million Cases'
26	20 August 2020	The Wall Street Journal	'Covid-19 Hits India's Already Faltering Consumers Hardest'
27	21 August 2020	The Washington Post	'These Americans Came to India to Deepen Their Faith. They've Been Detained, Quarantined and Prosecuted'
28	7 October 2020	The Telegraph	'Public Health Experts Call for Caution as Daily Covid-19 Cases Drop in India'
29	13 October 2020	The Guardian	'Covid-19 Prompts "Enormous Rise" in Demand for Cheap Child Labour in India'
30	15 October 2020	The New York Times	'What Happens When Covid-19 Meets Toxic Air? India Is About to Find Out'
31	19 October 2020	The Telegraph	'India "over Covid-19 Peak" as Nation Posts Lowest Death Toll for Three Months'
32	12 November 2020	The Telegraph	'Covid Plunges India into Recession for First Time in History'
33	12 November 2020	BBC News	'Delhi's Covid Cases Spike as Temperatures Drop and Pollution Rises'
34	23 November 2020	BBC News	'Covid: "Entire Families in Hospital after Coronavirus Surge"'

35	27 November 2020	The New York Times	'India's Economy Shrinks Sharply as Covid-19 Slams Small Businesses'
36	15 December 2020	The New York Times	'The Virus Trains: How Lockdown Chaos Spread Covid-19 across India'
37	28 December 2020	The Wall Street Journal	'What's Worse Than 2020 in America?'
38	4 January 2021	BBC News	'Covaxin: Concern over "rushed" Approval for India Covid Jab'
39	1 February 2021	The Telegraph	'India Registers Record Fall in Covid Cases amid Hopes Pandemic Is Finally Retreating'
40	15 March 2021	The New York Times	'How Do You Vaccinate 1.3 Billion People?'
41	25 March 2021	The Washington Post	'Massive Second Wave of Infections Is Emerging in India, Pitting the Virus against the Vaccine Rollout'
42	1 April 2021	BBC News	'Coronavirus Update: India Is Facing a "Severe, Intensive" Second Wave'
43	2 April 2021	The Guardian	'The World's Poorest Countries Are at India's Mercy for Vaccines. It's Unsustainable'
44	9 April 2021	The New York Times	'Complacency and Missteps Deepen a Covid-19 Crisis in India'
45	14 April 2021	Time	'Officially, India Has the World's Second-Worst COVID-19 Outbreak. Unofficially, It's Almost Certainly the Worst'
46	16 April 2021	The New York Times	'Covid-19 Pushes India's Middle Class toward Poverty'
47	16 April 2021	The Telegraph	"'The Pandora's Box Is Open Now': Doctors Reveal Horror of India's "Double Mutant" Second Wave'

48	20 April 2021	The Washington Post	'India's Devastating Outbreak Is Driving the Global Coronavirus Surge'
49	21 April 2021	The New York Times	'India's Health System Cracks Under the Strain as Coronavirus Cases Surge'
50	23 April 2021	Time	'"This Is Hell." Prime Minister Modi's Failure to Lead Is Deepening India's COVID-19 Crisis'
51	23 April 2021	BBC News	'Covid-19: Delhi Hospitals Run out of Oxygen Supplies'
52	23 April 2021	The New York Times	'India Scrambles to Supply Oxygen as Covid-19 Patients Gasp for Breath'
53	23 April 2021	The Guardian	'The Guardian View on Modi's Mistakes: A Pandemic That Is Out of Control'
54	25 April 2021	The Wall Street Journal	'India's Covid Surge Is Most Ferocious Yet. "Spreading Like Wildfire."'
55	26 April 2021	The New York Times	'Amid Second Virus Wave, the World Responds to India's Distress Call'
56	26 April 2021	The Wall Street Journal	'India Accused of Censorship for Blocking Social Media Criticism amid Covid Surge'
57	27 April 2021	BBC News	'India Covid: Delhi Builds Makeshift Funeral Pyres as Deaths Climb'
58	28 April 2021	Time	'India's COVID-19 Crisis Is Spiraling Out of Control. It Didn't Have to Be This Way'
59	29 April 2021	The Washington Post	'In India's Devastating Coronavirus Surge, Anger at Modi Grows'
60	4 May 2021	BBC News	'Covid in Varanasi: Anger Rises as Coronavirus Rages in Modi's Constituency'

61	4 May 2021	BBC News	'India Covid: Opposition Calls for Full National Lockdown'
62	7 May 2021	The Guardian	'Covid Rips through Rural India's Threadbare Healthcare System'
63	8 May 2021	BBC News	'India's Covid Crisis Delivers a Blow to Brand Modi'
64	25 May 2021	The New York Times	'Indian Police Visit Twitter Offices as Modi Goes on Pandemic Offense'
65	28 May 2021	Time	'Modi Never Bought Enough COVID-19 Vaccines for India. Now the Whole World Is Paying'
66	30 May 2021	The Guardian	'Vietnam Says New Covid Variant Is Hybrid of India and U.K. Strains'

INDEX

'Song of Lawino,' 138
'White Man's Burden,' 42

Agence France-Presse (AFP), 15
Agence Havas, 16
Allied Powers, 43
Alpha variant, 110
Al Qaeda, 56, 58
Ambedkar, Dr B.R., ix, xiv, 37, 38, 39, 40
Angus Maddison Research, 73
artificial intelligence (AI), 23, 74, 77, 147
Associated Press (AP), 15
Associate Press of India, 24
AstraZeneca, 105, 106, 139
Axis Powers, 43

Bahini, Mukti, 46
Bangladesh Liberation War, 46
BBC, 49, 51, 52, 53, 54, 56, 57, 58, 66, 67, 69, 70, 72, 77, 81, 94, 107, 108, 109, 110, 112, 130, 154, 155, 156, 157, 158, 159
Bengal famine, xv
Bevin, Ernest, 31
Bharatiya Janata Party (BJP), 61, 93
Brazil, 3, 103
Britain, 1, 22, 28, 29, 41, 64, 70, 71, 73, 146
Burma, 31, 32
Bush, George, 62

Calcutta, 51
Chandrayaan-2, 69
Chandrayaan-3, 68, 69, 71, 72, 78
Chauhan, Jagjit Singh, 52

Check Point, 108, 109
China, 19, 53, 63, 87, 92, 111, 112, 114, 115, 126, 127, 128, 129, 130, 134, 152
Chinese Communist Party, 21
Christianity, 6, 12, 145
Christys, Patrick, 70, 72
Churchill, Winston, xiii, 41, 66, 91
cobra, 125, 126, 131, 132
Cold War, 21, 43, 50, 145
Collyer, Gordon, xiii, 29
Columbus, Christopher, 4, 9
Congo, 8, 9
Congress, 38, 39, 61, 92, 149
Covid-19, ix, xiv, xv, xvi, xvii, xviii, 67, 68, 80, 82, 86, 87, 88, 89, 90, 91, 92, 93, 94, 95, 96, 97, 98, 99, 100, 101, 102, 103, 104, 105, 106, 107, 109, 110, 111, 112, 113, 115, 116, 117, 118, 119, 120, 125, 127, 128, 130, 132, 140, 152, 153, 155, 156, 157, 158
Covishield, 105, 106, 107, 108
CoWIN, 106, 107

da Gama, Vasco, 5, 7, 12, 68
Delta variant, 109
digital media, x, 146, 147
Durant, Will, 73, 74

East India Company, 5
East Pakistan, 45, 46, 47
Eden, Anthony, 28
Elite Space Club, 63, 65, 66
Emergency, 52
evangelization, 12

Farage, Nigel, 71, 72

Galwan Valley, 129
Gandhi, Indira, 45, 47, 51, 52, 53, 61
Gandhi, Rajmohan, 86
Garib Kalyan Rojgar Abhiyan, 122
Global South, 23, 115, 125, 151, 153
Global Times, 112
Guardian, The, 11, 12, 49, 56, 59, 71, 72, 88, 89, 90, 91, 92, 94, 98, 100, 110, 114
Gulf News, 80, 81, 84, 126

Haldeman H.R., 47, 51
Hamas, 57
Haridas, Sharnaya, 65
Havas, Charles-Louis, 16
Heng Kim Song, 66
Heslehurst, Aaron, 69, 70, 72
Hindu Mahasabha, 38

Huffpost, 65
Hyderabad, x, xiii, 28, 29, 30, 31, 34, 44
hydroxychloroquine, 113, 128, 130

Independence, ix, 5, 32, 37, 38, 40, 44, 45, 71, 73
Indian Council of Medical Research (ICMR), 128, 130
Indian Institute of Mass Communication (IIMC), 117, 118, 119
Indian Railways, 128
Indian Space Research Organisation (ISRO), 67, 68, 70, 76, 77, 78, 79
Iron Curtain, 27

Jaish-e-Mohammed, 56
Jan Dhan Bank, 122
Jio, 77, 78, 151
Junagadh, 34

Kashmir, 29, 34, 54, 57, 58, 155
Kasim Razvi, 30
Kerala, 92, 125, 126, 127
Kissinger, Henry, 47, 49, 50, 51
Kumbh Mela, 95

Ladakh, 127, 129
Laden, Osama Bin, 58
Lashkar-e-Tayyaba, 56
Lawino, 138, 143
Leopold II, 8
Line of Actual Control, 115, 129
Los Angeles Times, xv, 84

Mahindra, Anand, 72
Malle, Louis, 51
Mangalyaan, 65, 67, 68, 137
Matta, Fernando Reyes, 2, 22
MGNREGA, 122
Modi, Narendra, ix, xvi, xviii, 13, 60, 61, 80, 91, 92, 93, 99, 101, 109, 111, 116, 127, 129, 133, 134, 135, 136, 137, 154, 155, 156, 158, 159
Mookerjee, Dr Shyama Prasad, 38
Morrison, Patt, xv, 84
Multidimensional Poverty Index (MPI), 75
Musharraf, Parvez, 55

Nehru, Jawaharlal, ix, xi, xiv, 25, 26, 27, 37, 38, 39, 40
New York Associated Press, 17, 18
New York Times, The, xvi, xvii, 11, 12, 49, 56, 58, 59, 65, 66,

68, 79, 93, 94, 97, 101, 102, 103, 104, 133, 134, 135, 136, 137, 154, 155, 156, 157, 158, 159
Nitin Srivastava, 69
Nixon, Richard, 47, 50, 51
new world information and communication order (NWICO), 150, 152, 153
new world information order (NWIO), 2, 23, 150, 152

O Estado, 3
Okot p'Bitek, 138
Operation Parakram, 55
Operation Searchlight, 46
Oxford Poverty and Human Development Initiative (OPHI), 75

Pakistan, xiv, 25, 33, 34, 43, 44, 45, 46, 47, 54, 55, 56, 58, 59, 60, 77, 133
Panikkar, K.M., 144, 145
Panthik Party, 38
Partition, 33, 34, 91
Patel, Sardar Vallabhbhai, ix, xii, xiii, xiv, 29, 30, 32, 33, 34, 35, 36, 37, 39, 40, 61, 83
Phantom India, 51
Pilani, xiv, 33, 34, 35
PM Kisan Yojana, 122
Pompeo, Mike, 111
Powell, Colin, 55
Press Trust of India (PTI), 20, 24, 25, 26, 27, 28, 43

Radcliffe, Sir Cyril, 33
Rahman, Sheikh Mujibur, 45
Ray, Satyajit, 51
Reuter, Paul, 16, 19
Reuters, xiv, 15, 16, 17, 18, 22, 24, 25, 26, 27, 28, 43, 56, 62, 63, 64, 110, 141
Rosenthal, Andrew, 66
Russia–Ukraine war, 77

Sanyal, Sanjeev, 97, 98
saree, 142, 143
Serum Research Institute of India, 106, 114
Shramik Special trains, 97, 128
Silicon Valley, 147
Simpson, John, 57
Singh, Sardar Baldev, 38
Singh, Surendra Pal, 52
Smith, Anthony, 1, 6, 10, 12, 16, 19, 20
social media, 23, 27, 87, 96, 133, 148, 149
South Africa, 30, 81

South America, 1, 18
Spanish Flu, xiv, xv, 80, 81, 82, 83, 84, 85, 86, 87, 88, 89
Spinney, Laura, xv, 83, 84, 87
Srinivasan, Kasturi, 25
Stanley, Henry Morton, 8, 9, 10, 12
Suriname, 1, 2, 3, 14, 146
S. Viswam, 151

Telegrafnoye Agentstvo Sovetskogo Soyuza (TASS), 21, 129
Economist, The, 62, 83
Netherlands, the, 1, 18, 106
Third World, 2, 14, 15, 22, 50, 64, 105, 144, 146
Trump, Donald, 111, 112, 130

Uganda, 143
UK, xii, xiv, xvii, 4, 28, 29, 31, 32, 33, 51, 52, 53, 64, 70, 71, 72, 88, 98, 103, 104, 105, 106, 107, 108, 109, 110, 113, 139
United Nations (UN), 26, 28, 75, 106
USA, xii, xiv, 2, 4, 5, 8, 11, 17, 18, 23, 55, 58, 64, 93, 98, 103, 105, 107, 108, 109, 110, 111, 112, 113, 115, 136, 139, 141, 149

Vaccine Maitri, 114
vasudhaiva kutumbakam, 113

Western Associated Press, 17
WHO, 87, 98, 102, 108, 110, 112, 130
Wolff, Bernhard, 16, 17
Wolffs Telegraphisches Bureau (WTB), 16
World War I, 20, 82, 86, 87
World War II, 2, 20, 24, 44, 64
Wuhan, 110, 111, 112

Xinhua, 21